The Complete Guide
To Texas Lawn Care

# THE COMPLETE GUIDE TO
# TEXAS LAWN CARE

## BY DR. WILLIAM E. KNOOP

*Editor:*
Rita Miller


*Illustrations:*
Mike Lee


*Design:*
Don Mulkey


*Photographs:*
Used by permission of:
Dr. William Knoop
Dr. James Reinert
Bob Starkowsky
H.A. Turney

TG Press
P.O. Box 9005
Waco, Texas 76714

Library of Congress Catalog Card Number: 85-051942.
ISBN: 0-914641-03-4 (cloth)
ISBN: 0-914641-04-2 (paperback)
Printed in Japan by Dai Nippon Printing Co. Ltd. through DNP (America), Inc.

To my wife, Elaine, for her help and constant support.

# TABLE OF CONTENTS

# INTRODUCTION

A well-kept home lawn is truely a thing of beauty and a continual source of pride to its owner. In a very practical sense, the lawn and its turfgrasses serve to hold the soil around a house in place and to prevent erosion, but the real value of the lawn also must be measured aesthetically.

Most people are susceptible to first impressions and your lawn can make a major contribution to the first impression people have as they approach your home—either as guests or, possibly, as prospective home buyers.

If you have an established lawn and you simply want to improve its quality with a good maintenance program, you can get the "nuts and bolts" from the "Quick Reference Guides" at the back of the book. From there, you will be referred to specific chapters for more detailed information.

If you need to establish a new lawn or renovate an old one, start with the information dealing with selecting the right turfgrass in Chapter 1 and read Chapters 3 and 4 for more help.

The right turfgrass in the right place is basic to a successful lawn. The first step is to review the tables at the end of the first chapter and pick out which turfgrass seems to fit your needs. It is not likely that any one grass will meet your needs completely, but pick the one that comes closest. After that, read about all the varieties of that particular turfgrass and narrow down your choice.

One of the hardest issues to deal with is trying to decide which turfgrass to use when a new lawn will be partly shaded, since so few turfgrasses do well in the shade.

Remember grasses like St. Augustine and zoysia that grow well in the shade also do well in the sun. Although it's a winter grass, tall fescue also will do well if it gets a lot of "tender loving care" in the summer.

**Bermudagrass comes in several different varieties and is widely used for Texas lawns.**

# I

# THE
# TURFGRASSES

There are many types of grasses which grow well in Texas and choosing one for your home landscape isn't necessarily a simple task. There are many factors you must consider in selecting the right turfgrass for your needs, including environmental conditions, maintenance requirements, expense and personal preferences.

Before making a choice, though, you should know a little something about the many turfgrasses that will do well in Texas. The major types you'll probably consider are bermudagrass, St. Augustinegrass, zoysiagrass, buffalograss, tall fescue, centipedegrass and Kentucky bluegrass.

## BERMUDAGRASS

All the bermudagrasses trace their origins back to Africa. They are warm-season grasses that go dormant with cool fall weather and "green up" with the return of warm spring weather. It generally takes soil temperatures in the 60s to get bermuda going in the spring. None of the bermuda varieties have any significant tolerance of shade. The bermudagrasses are very aggressive as a group, spreading both by rhizomes and stolons. If you grow one of these grasses you will need to

1

edge sidewalks and gardens, and trim around trees, shrubs, buildings and fences almost constantly. The bermudagrasses as a group have few disease or insect problems. The following are the major varieties of bermudagrasses.

**COMMON:** This is a fairly wide-bladed bermudagrass which offers a big advantage in that it can be established from seed. It has low maintenance requirements and will survive on minimal amounts of water and fertilizer. The best height of cut for common bermudagrass is 1½ inches and it can be maintained at slightly lower heights if it is cut more frequently. This grass does not tend to be a thatch producer but production of unsightly seed heads can be a problem, especially for those of you with allergies. There is very little Common bermudagrass sod available because it is so easy to start from seed. Common bermuda is used for many home lawns, athletic fields, golf course fairways, parks and other moderate maintenance areas.

**TIFGREEN (328):** This is one of the smallest leafed hybrid bermudagrasses available. It has an ideal cutting height in the ¼- to ½-inch range, but requires high levels of fertility and water to perform well. It also tends to be a thatch producer, especially if mowed too high. Tifgreen 328 is best suited for use on golf course putting greens where it is cut nearly every day and can receive the necessary level of maintenance. Tifgreen is a very aggressive, rapid spreading grass and for that reason it has been widely grown as sod for the home market. Before buying this grass, the homeowner should be aware of its demanding maintenance needs.

**TIFWAY (419):** Tifway is a true hybrid that has a slightly wider leaf blade than Tifgreen, but is not nearly as wide as Common. The best cutting height for this bermuda is ½ to 1 inch, but like 328 it also can develop thatch problems if it's over-fertilized and over-watered. For the homeowner who wants that "putting green" look for his lawn, this is the grass to consider. It can be established by using either sprigs or sod and is grown primarily on fairways, tees, athletic fields and occasionally on home lawns.

**TEXTURF 10:** This grass is a "selection" of Common bermuda. It was selected because it has more of a horizontal growth habit than Common bermuda and tends to make a thicker lawn at a mowing height around 1 inch. It is a great grass for a home lawn. It also could be used for fairways, tees and athletic fields and can be established by sprigging or sodding.

**MIDIRON:** This is a bermuda that was developed by Kansas State University and is used for all the same purposes as Common bermuda. It looks much like the Common variety but tends to stay green a little longer in the fall and green up a little earlier in the spring. It's only available as sod and sprigs. Midiron has superior cold tolerance.

**U3:** This is a hybrid bermuda that can be established from seed, but it doesn't come true from seed. The resulting turf looks a lot like Common bermuda but has superior cold tolerance.

# ST. AUGUSTINEGRASS

This turfgrass is native to the West Indies and our Guif Coast and is widely grown in the warm, humid parts of the United States. Its best attribute is its outstanding shade tolerance. St. Augustine usually is established by sod, but plugs of the newer varieties are available now. It spreads quickly by stolons, but has low wear tolerance, which may make it undesirable for highly used lawns. All St. Augustines have wider leaf blades than most other turfgrasses. The following is a brief description of the major St. Augustine varieties.

**COMMON:** This is by far the most widely used St. Augustine. It is as cold tolerant as any other St. Augustine, but is susceptible to St. Augustine Decline (SAD) and to chinch bug damage.

**FLORATAM:** This is a St. Augustine released by the University of Florida and Texas A&M University. While it is resistant to SAD and to chinch bugs it does not have nearly the cold tolerance of Common St. Augustine and should not be grown too far from the Gulf Coast area. Floratam does not have the shade tolerance that Common or Raleigh varieties have.

**RALEIGH:** This is a North Carolina State University release that has SAD resistance. Raleigh looks much like Texas Common St. Augustine and is almost as cold tolerant.

**SEVILLE:** This is a dwarf type St. Augustine that does not have the cold tolerance of the Common or Raleigh varieties and should be used only in the southernmost parts of the South. It does have SAD resistance.

**St. Augustinegrass has wider blades than most other grasses and will grow in many shady areas.**

From time to time, new St. Augustine varieties will become available. To evaluate a new variety, ask the following questions:

1. Is it more cold tolerant than Common?
2. Is it SAD resistant?
3. Is it chinch bug resistant?
4. Is it fine-textured?

The answers to these questions should help you decide if a new variety of St. Augustine is better than the old ones.

# ZOYSIAGRASS

This turfgrass is native to the Orient. It is not as shade tolerant as St. Augustine but is much more shade tolerant than bermuda. Zoysia spreads by both rhizomes and stolons but has a fairly low growth rate.

**Zoysiagrass (top) is well-adapted to Texas, but is not commonly grown. Buffalograss (bottom) is native to the state and has low maintenance requirements.**

If established by plugs, placed every 12 inches, it may take as long as two seasons to fill in completely. Common bermuda and other traditional ''weedy'' species can be a serious problem in a newly zoysia-plugged lawn.

Other than plugging, the use of sod is the best way to start a zoysia lawn. The lawn should be completely covered with sod instead of just using sod strips. Zoysia is more winter hardy than bermuda or St. Augustine.

Two zoysia varieties usually are available: Emerald and Meyer. Emerald has a much finer leaf blade than Meyer and can form a very dense, dark green lawn. The leaf blade of Meyer might be just a little wider than that of Common bermuda, but it can form a dense turf.

Both zoysia varieties have a fairly low lateral growth rate and, for that reason, it may take growers twice as long to produce zoysia sod as it does to produce bermuda or St. Augustine sod—and that increases the price. Zoysia is a good southern grass that has been ''overlooked'' because of its price and unavailability. The poor results gained from attempting to establish zoysia from plugs also has hurt its image.

# BUFFALOGRASS

This is the only turfgrass that is native to the North American Great Plains, from Texas to Canada. It is a warm-season turfgrass that spreads by stolons. Buffalograss has fine leaf blades that are a blue-green in color. It will not form a turf as dense as bermuda, but if left unmowed, it will not grow to more than 4 or 5 inches in height. It can survive extreme drought conditions but may turn brown during dry summer periods, only to green up again when it rains.

Buffalograss is established from seeds that are called burrs. The seed is larger than other grass seed and overall production is low, making the price of buffalograss on the high side. Buffalograss is the only turfgrass that is dioecious, which means there are both male and female plants. The male flower is produced on the end of a stalk while the female flower is produced at the base of the plant.

Buffalograss has no particular insect or disease problems. Its biggest enemies are, perhaps, over-watering and over-fertilizing.

# TALL FESCUE

This is a cool-season, or northern, turfgrass that originated in Europe and is tough enough to take southern summers if it is managed right. Tall fescue is one of the most heat- and drought-tolerant of the northern grasses. It is a ''bunch'' grass, which means it spreads by tillers. And that means you have to do very little edging. Also, the fescue won't invade any flower or shrub beds.

Fescue's greatest plus is its ability to grow well in fairly dense shade and survive the winters without any problems. And, best of all, it

**Tall fescue (top) is a cool-season grass that is susceptible to hot summer weather in the southern half of the state. Centipede looks a lot like St. Augustine but has smaller leaves.**

will stay green all winter. Tall fescue will grow at its highest rate during spring and fall. The long, hot summers give tall fescue its biggest test. If the growing point of the plant, which is near the soil surface, gets too hot the whole plant will turn brown. This is a natural process, which the plant uses to escape from heat damage. If the dormant period isn't too prolonged, the plant will renew growth when cool weather returns. A good watering every three or four days during the summer should be enough to keep it green. The water helps keep the soil cool. Any more watering than that increases the chances that diseases will develop. Mowing at 2 inches or higher will help keep the growing point cooler.

The old standard tall fescue variety has been K-31 and it's still available. There are, however, several new varieties that have finer leaf blades, and improved heat and shade tolerance. They are Olympic, Rebel, Falcon and Houndog.

Tall fescue has no special disease or insect problems.

Over-watered tall fescue lawns, however, usually do have helminthosporium problems during the summer.

# CENTIPEDEGRASS

This turfgrass, a native of China and Southeast Asia, looks a lot like St. Augustine but has smaller leaves and is a little lighter green in color. It spreads by stolons and is established primarily by seed. Centipede has a fairly slow rate of establishment. Only zoysia has a slower rate of spread. Centipedegrass is best suited to sandy acid soils and may have severe iron chlorosis if grown on heavy alkaline soils.

Centipede takes winter better than St. Augustine and has low wear tolerance. It requires less mowing than bermudagrass or St. Augustine and is moderately shade tolerant.

# KENTUCKY BLUEGRASS

This is a cool-season, northern turfgrass from Europe that is grown more than any other grass. It may be grown in the extreme Upper South or in higher elevations that cool off at night. It does best at temperatures around 75 degrees. Kentucky bluegrass spreads primarily by rhizomes and is established from sod or seed. There are a great number of Kentucky bluegrasses sold and it is recommended that a mixture of three or four different ones be used.

The following graphs help compare the strengths and weaknesses of the various turfgrasses. They should help you decide which grass best meets your needs.

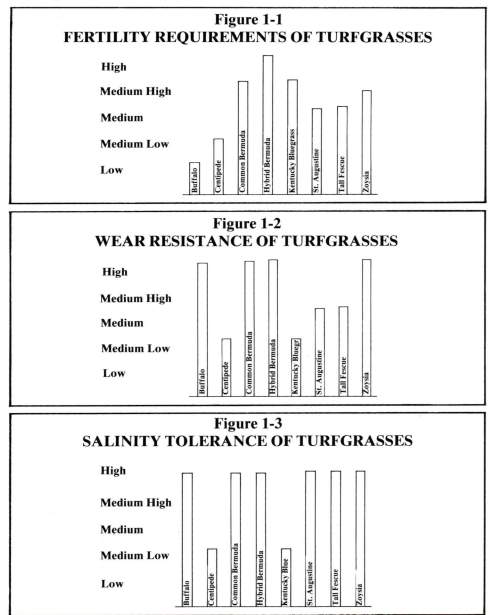

**Figure 1-1**
**FERTILITY REQUIREMENTS OF TURFGRASSES**

**Figure 1-2**
**WEAR RESISTANCE OF TURFGRASSES**

**Figure 1-3**
**SALINITY TOLERANCE OF TURFGRASSES**

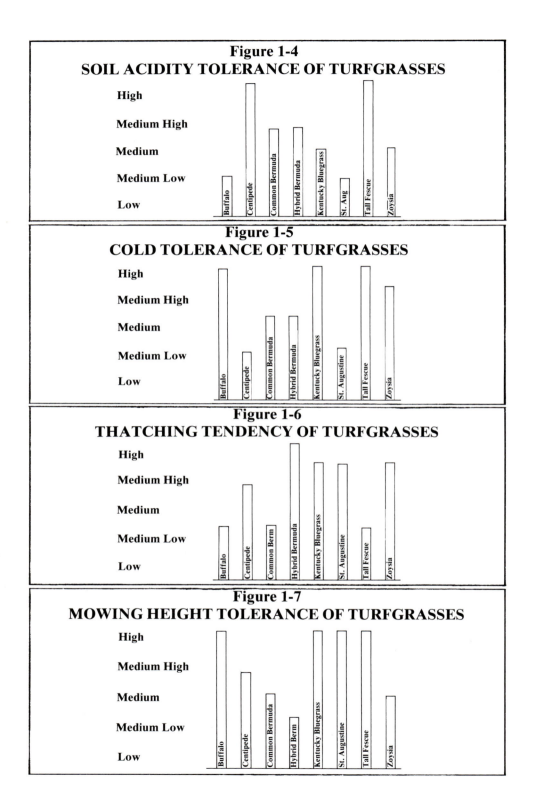

**Figure 1-4**
**SOIL ACIDITY TOLERANCE OF TURFGRASSES**

**Figure 1-5**
**COLD TOLERANCE OF TURFGRASSES**

**Figure 1-6**
**THATCHING TENDENCY OF TURFGRASSES**

**Figure 1-7**
**MOWING HEIGHT TOLERANCE OF TURFGRASSES**

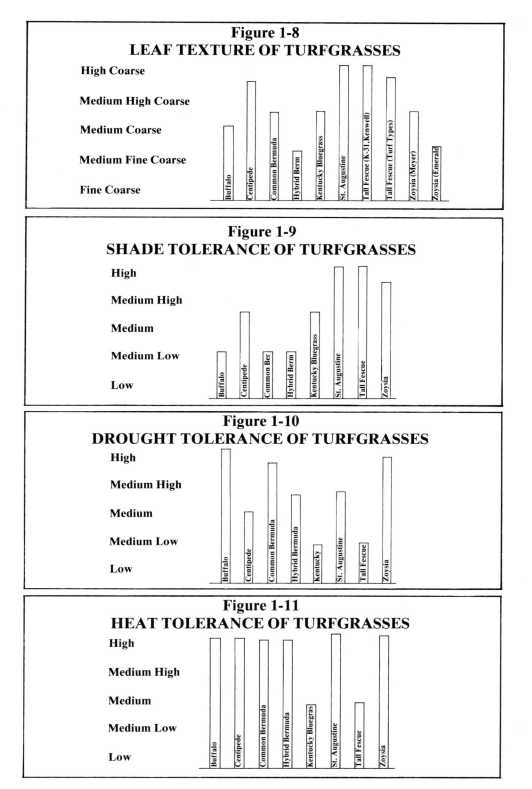

# II
## TURFGRASS GROWTH AND ESTABLISHMENT

I f you're like most people, you've probably never given much thought to the various parts of the grass plant and what they do. But you should take the time to become familiar with them because they help determine how to properly maintain your lawn. So let's look at each component of the turfgrass plant, beginning with the roots.

## THE ROOT SYSTEM

The primary function of the root system is to draw water and nutrients into the plant. Anything that affects the health of the root system has a direct effect on the health of the rest of the plant.

Root growth is sensitive to soil temperatures. The southern grass plants' root systems grow best when soil temperatures are between 80 and 90 degrees, while the growth of the northern grasses is favored by soil temperatures of 50 to 60 degrees. This relationship between soil temperature and root growth helps explain why traditional northern turfgrasses, like tall fescue and perennial ryegrass, have problems during the hot summer months when soil temperatures are at their highest.

The amount of air in the soil also has a direct effect on the growth of the root system. Roots take in oxygen and give off gasses such as carbon dioxide. As a soil is trafficked, the amount of space available for air is reduced slowly. This process is called soil

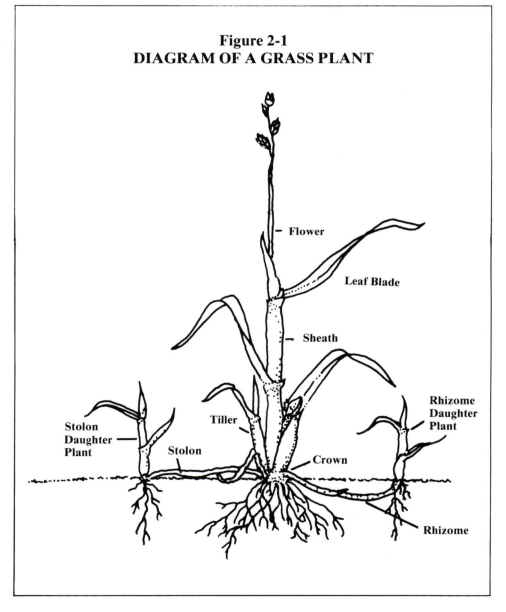

**Figure 2-1**
**DIAGRAM OF A GRASS PLANT**

compaction. Also, any process that keeps the soil too wet for an extended period makes soil air levels too low for good root growth.

Many people find it surprising that the height at which you mow your grass affects the growth of the root system. A grass plant tries to maintain a balance between its aboveground and below-ground parts. In other words, a certain sized root system can only provide enough water and nutrients for a leaf system of a corresponding size. In reverse, a certain sized leaf system can manufacture only enough food to support a root system of a corresponding size. When either the leaf or root system of the plant is reduced, such as when the leaf system is cut back during mowing, the other system is reduced in an effort to achieve a balance. When the plant is mowed, root growth essentially stops until the plant has grown more leaves. Basically, leaf growth has priority over root growth, which sometimes can cause problems.

The priority for leaf growth to the detriment of root growth is most apparent when a lawn is over-fertilized with a soluble nitrogen, making it very possible to have a lawn that produces lots of leaf growth and almost no root growth. To avoid this possibility, use only recommended rates of nitrogen.

A deficiency of any of the so called "essential" plant nutrients eventually will have an effect on root growth but the relationship between nitrogen and potassium has a particularly dramatic effect. Root growth is generated by increases in the amount of potassium supplied to the plant while leaf growth is favored by increased amounts of nitrogen. The nitrogen-potassium ratio in fertilizer recommendations take this relationship into consideration.

The grass root is surrounded by what is called "the soil solution." Nutrients that are available naturally in the soil and those obtained from fertilizer pass through this solution to the root. Many nutrients and some irrigation waters can raise the salt level in the soil system, which can cause serious injury to root systems.

There are many other factors that can have a negative effect on root growth, including extremely high or low pH, the over-application of pre-emergent herbicides, an excessive thatch layer, insects, nematodes and root diseases.

**Table 2-1**
**TYPES OF LATERAL STEMS**

| Variety | Types of Lateral Stems | | |
| --- | --- | --- | --- |
| | Rhizome | Stolon | Tiller |
| Bermudagrass | x | x | |
| St. Augustine | | x | |
| Zoysiagrass | | x | |
| Centipedegrass | | x | |
| Buffalograss | | x | |
| Perennial Ryegrass | | | x |
| Tall Fescue | | | x |
| Bluegrass | x | | |

**Figure 2-2**
**DIAGRAM OF STOLON**
**(St. Augustine, Centipede, Buffalograss, Bermuda)**

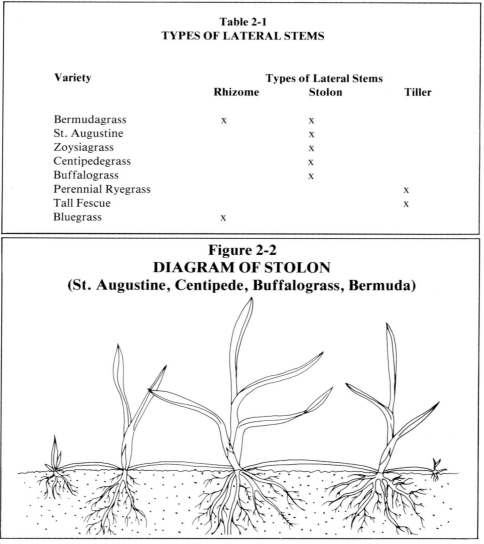

# CROWN AND LATERAL STEMS

The crown, also called the "growing point," of the grass plant is located close to the soil surface. The primary roots, lateral stems and leaves all arise from the crown. (See Figure 2-1.) This area of the plant is very sensitive to heat, especially in the northern turfgrasses. The optimum temperature range for the upper parts of the southern

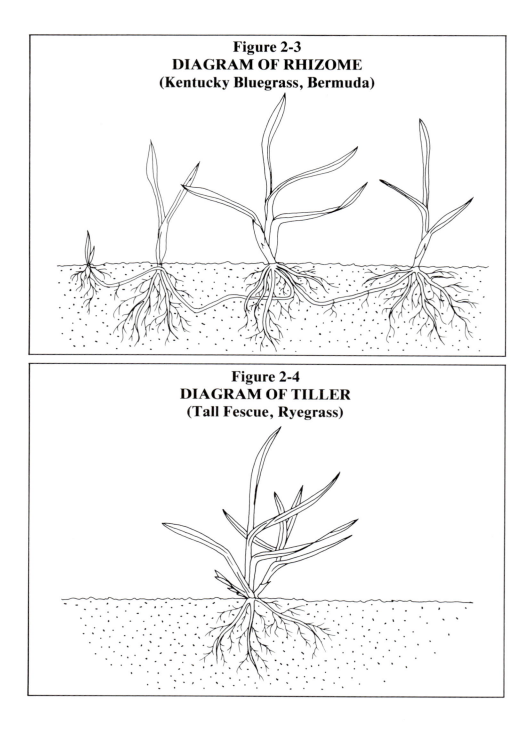

**Figure 2-3**
**DIAGRAM OF RHIZOME**
**(Kentucky Bluegrass, Bermuda)**

**Figure 2-4**
**DIAGRAM OF TILLER**
**(Tall Fescue, Ryegrass)**

turfgrasses is in the 85- to 95-degree range while northern turfgrasses do best when air temperatures are from 65 to 75 degrees. As the crown of a northern turfgrass, such as tall fescue, is heated above its optimum temperature range as it would be on a summer day, the growth process begins to slow down. If the crown gets hot enough, the plant may stop growing completely. Aboveground parts may turn brown. The plant has not died, but has entered what is called "summer dormancy." If high temperatures do not persist for too long the plant will renew growth when cooler weather returns. The length of time the plant can remain dormant has a great deal to do with its "state of health" at the time it goes dormant. The relative higher heights of cut for turfgrasses like tall fescue take advantage of a heavy leaf canopy to insulate the plant's crown and help keep it cool. The crown and the lateral stems are the "over-wintering" parts of the southern turfgrass plants. There are three types of lateral stems produced by various turfgrasses. (See Table 2-1.) A stolon (Figure 2-2) is a lateral stem that grows along the surface of the soil. As the stolon grows, every so often it produces a node. A node becomes the crown of a new plant and soon produces its own stolons. A rhizome (Figure 2-3) serves the same function as a stolon, but grows below the soil surface. A tiller (Figure 2-4) is a very short lateral stem that produces a new plant close to the crown of the parent plant.

## LEAVES AND FLOWERS

The leaf of the turfgrass plant, as with all other plants, is the primary site for photosynthesis—the process by which the plant converts light energy into food materials called carbohydrates. Many turfgrass diseases affect the leaves of the plant. The lesions, or dead spots, the diseases may cause reduce the amount of leaf area available for photosynthesis. This, in turn, reduces carbohydrate production and in time the health of the plant will be affected.

The flowers of most turfgrass plants are usually never seen but some grasses, such as some bermudas, have the ability to produce what are considered unsightly seed heads almost overnight after mowing. There is no real way to prevent this from happening but a good balanced fertility program will help.

# III
# SOILS
# AND
# THEIR
# MODIFICATION

The soil is a complex mixture of organic and inorganic materials. It serves as a major source of both the water and nutrients needed for growth of the turfgrass plant.

## SOIL STRUCTURE

Soil is made up of minerals called sand, silt and clay and the difference between these three is both physical and chemical. Physically, they are different in size. (See Table 3-1.) When a soil is tested, you determine how much sand, silt and clay it contains by using a set of sieves. The resulting percentages place the soil in what is called a soil texture group, such as loam, clay loam and sandy loam. For example, if a soil contains about 50 percent sand, 30 percent silt and 20 percent clay it's called a loam. Clay loam has about 20 percent sand, 20 percent silt and 60 percent clay. A sandy loam has 60 percent sand, 20 percent silt and 20 percent clay. Most consider a sandy loam to be the best soil texture for a lawn because it has good drainage and good nutrient-holding characteristics.

The most important direct effects of soil structure on lawns is the rate at which water enters the soil, the amount of water the soil holds

**Soils which have a very high clay content may develop large cracks during dry periods. Good irrigation practices will keep this from happening.**

and the rate at which water drains through the soil. As the percentage of sand in a soil increases, water will enter it more quickly, it will hold less water and the water moves down through the soil faster.

Thus, sandy soils tend to be very droughty and must be watered frequently. Clay soils dramatically slow down water infiltration and increase water retention. However, they also are poorly drained and puddles develop after even a short rain. Generally, turfgrasses form deeper roots in sandy soils than they do in clay soils. (See Table 3-2 for information on water infiltration rates in specific soils.)

Several different kinds of clay minerals are found in soils and one particular clay, called montmorillonite, can cause some rather serious problems. It is found in many soils and shrinks when dried. If your soil has a high percentage of this clay, cracks measuring several inches across and several feet deep may open in the soil during dry periods. When this happens on a lawn area that is used for play, it's very easy to turn an ankle or suffer even worse injuries. Good irrigation practices will prevent these cracks.

**Table: 3-1**
**SOIL MINERAL SIZE**

| Soil Mineral | Size (m.m.) |
|---|---|
| Sand | 2.0 to 0.05 |
| Silt | 0.05 50 0.002 |
| Clay | below 0.002 |

**Table 3-2**
**INFILTRATION RATES OF OVERHEAD**
**APPLIED WATER THROUGH SOILS**

| Soil Texture | Infiltration Rate (Inches/Hour) |
|---|---|
| Sand | 1 - 10 |
| Sandy Loam | 0.5 - 3 |
| Loam | 0.3 - 0.8 |
| Clay Loam | 0.1 - 0.6 |
| Clay | 0.01 - 0.4 |

The shrinking and swelling of a soil also often have a negative effect on house foundations and the soil must be kept at an even moisture level around the home to prevent problems. Soils that contain this "shrinking" clay do a considerable amount of rising and dropping between wet and dry periods. A low spot one year may be a high spot the next year.

# SOIL CHEMISTRY

The ability of a soil to hold and supply nutrients to a plant depends on the amount of clay and, to some degree, the amount of organic matter it contains. Both the clay particles and organic matter have a negative charge and since most plant nutrients have a positive charge, the nutrients are held to their surface for future use by the turfgrass plant. Soils very high in sand do not hold many nutrients, so fertilizer programs are more critical. As an extreme example, a lawn grown on a very sandy soil may need to be fertilized with small amounts of fertilizer every two or three weeks, while lawns grown on soils containing moderate amounts of clay can go as much a six weeks between fertilizer applications. (See Chapter 7 for more information on fertilizer requirements.)

# SOIL DRAINAGE

The lack of good soil drainage can be one of the worst continual problems a lawn can have. Grass roots simply won't grow in wet soils. Surface drainage may be adequate if the grade is at least 1 percent. This means that for water to run downhill, the slope should drop at least 1 foot for every 100 feet in distance or ½ foot for every 50 feet from the house. (See Figure 3-1.)

While surface drainage is important and will aid greatly in keeping the lawn from becoming water-logged, especially during periods of heavy rainfall, the internal drainage characteristics of a soil are just as important. There may be several reasons why a soil doesn't drain well internally. The most common cause is simply the high amount of clay in the soil. Clay holds water and the higher the percentage of clay in the soil, the more water is held and the poorer the drainage.

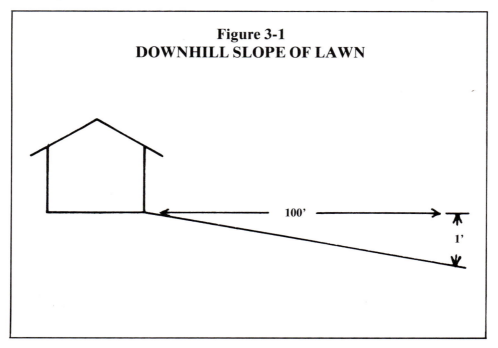

**Figure 3-1**
**DOWNHILL SLOPE OF LAWN**

**Some soils develop high and low spots and should be leveled by adding soil in the spring before the grass "greens up."**

Soils that are very high in calcium and/or sodium may tend to be poorly drained. These are two of the elements that may cause the soil to lose its desirable structure and, thus, its good drainage characteristics. If a soil has lost its structure because it is high in sodium, the addition of gypsum may improve internal drainage. Since gypsum is calcium sulfate, its application to a high calcium soil won't help. A soil test will determine if either sodium or calcium is a problem.

# SOIL pH

The pH of the soil has one very important effect on the growth of the lawn: it controls the availablilty of the nutrients in the soil. It doesn't matter if the nutrients are provided by the application of a liquid or dry fertilizer or if the nutrients are supplied by the decomposition of soil minerals, their availability to the grass plant is controlled to a large degree by the soil pH. (See Figure 3-2.) Most nutrients are available in the greatest amount when the soil's pH is around 6.5. The pH level also reduces the effectiveness of micro-organisms in the soil, which are needed to convert some plant nutrients from an unavailable form into a form the plant can use. These conversions are slower in both high and low pH soils. (Those micro-organisms also are responsible for the decomposition of thatch.)

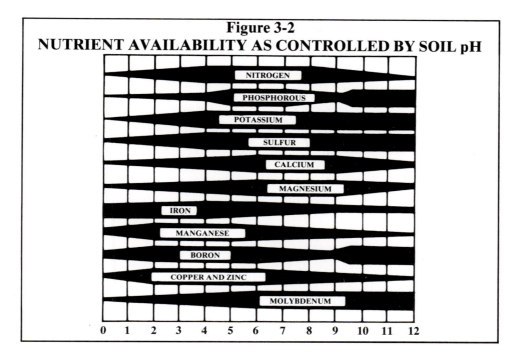

**Figure 3-2**
**NUTRIENT AVAILABILITY AS CONTROLLED BY SOIL pH**

    The most common nutrient problem associated with an excessively high or low pH is that of an iron deficiency. Many times there is enough iron in the soil, but it simply is not available to the plant. It is rare to have any minor nutrient problem that can be related directly to pH but if you do, the use of a fertilizer containing iron once or twice a year should help.

# PHYSICAL SOIL MODIFICATION

    The goal of physically modifying a soil is to provide better internal drainage. The most commonly used material to improve drainage is sand, which is available in many types and sizes. (See Figure 3-3.) Some sands are very fine and should not be used. An ideal sand particle should have a diameter of about ½ millimeter. This is a fairly coarse sand. Sands are sold under names like cement sand, mortar sand, sugar sand, bedding sand and foundation sand. The problem with these names is that they do not relate to any physical particle size and do not necessarily assure quality. The fine sands, when mixed with clay and dried out, can form a very hard surface.

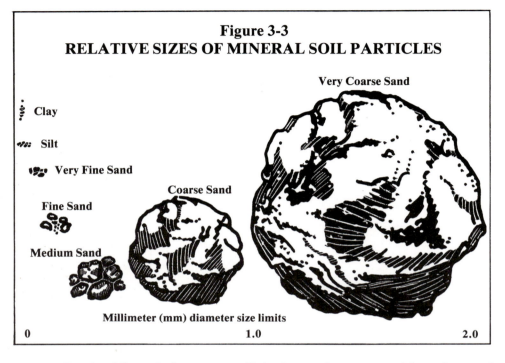

**Figure 3-3**
**RELATIVE SIZES OF MINERAL SOIL PARTICLES**

Very Coarse Sand

Clay

Silt

Very Fine Sand

Coarse Sand

Fine Sand

Medium Sand

Millimeter (mm) diameter size limits

0                                    1.0                                    2.0

To significantly improve soil drainage, large quantities of a good quality sand must be used. For example, if the soil to be modified is a clay loam that contains 20 percent sand, 20 percent silt and 60 percent clay, and it is mixed with an equal quantity of sand, the resulting soil would have a composition of 60 percent sand, 10 percent silt and 30 percent clay. This new soil will have better drainage, but it does take large amounts of sand to modify a clay soil. A few inches of sand spread over a soil and then rototilled into it probably won't improve drainage significantly. An ideal soil contains about 5 percent organic matter. Some soils that are high in clay and low in organic matter have poor drainage. Mixing organic matter into these soils may improve drainage just as much if not more than just adding sand does. Decomposed or composted organic matter should be used. Fresh organic matter is not as desirable because the organisms that decompose organic matter have a high nitrogen requirement. Thus, any plants growing in soils containing fresh organic matter usually have severe nitrogen deficiencies until the organic matter has decomposed.

Sand can be added to soils to enhance drainage (top), but you have to use large amounts for it to work. The first symptom of a salt problem is reduced growth, but as salt levels increase you can see a white deposit of salt on the soil surface (bottom).

**Table 3-3**
**AMOUNT OF GROUND OR DOLOMITIC LIMESTONE NEEDED PER 1,000 SQUARE FEET TO RAISE pH TO 6.5**

| | Soil Texture Class | | |
|---|---|---|---|
| Soil pH | Sand | Loam | Clay |
| 6.0 | 20 | 35 | 50 |
| 5.5 | 45 | 75 | 100 |
| 5.0 | 65 | 110 | 150 |
| 4.5 | 80 | 150 | 200 |
| 4.0 | 100 | 175 | 230 |

**Table 3-4**
**AMOUNT OF ELEMENTAL SULFUR NEEDED PER 1,000 SQUARE FEET TO LOWER pH TO 6.5**

| | Soil Texture Class | |
|---|---|---|
| Soil pH | Sandy | Clay |
| 8.5 | 35-45 | 45-60 |
| 8.0 | 25-35 | 35-50 |
| 7.5 | 10-15 | 20-25 |

# LAWN LEVELLING

From time to time, especially with a new lawn, it may be necessary and desirable to level the lawn by filling in the low spots. This process is done most easily in the spring, before the lawn "greens up."

The dormant lawn may be scalped to near the soil level. The next step is to spread the soil into the low spots. The scalping will make it easier to spread the soil. The same type of soil should be used that was used for the original lawn. Sand should not be used for levelling a lawn unless the existing soil is sand. The use of the same kind of soil and the loosening of the old soil surface should prevent layering. If layers are created in a soil, they tend to restrict the development of a deep root system.

# CHEMICAL SOIL MODIFICATION

If a soil test indicates that the pH is less than 6.5, an application of limestone usually is recommended. Limestone is calcium carbonate (CaCo2) and will supply calcium, a necessary nutrient, to the plant. If dolomitic limestone is used, magnesium as well as calcium is supplied. The higher the amount of clay in a soil, the more limestone is needed to change the pH. (See Table 3-3.)

Soils that have a pH higher than 6.5 may be modified with sulfur, which lowers pH. (See Table 3-4.) Three commonly used forms of sulfur are powder, flake and granular. The powder form works faster than the others but is more messy to use. One potential problem associated with the use of sulfur is that when sulfur is used and there is not good internal soil drainage, the soluble salt levels of the soil may be increased. This may be one reason why sulfur recommendations may not be very common. It probably is a good practice to make sure there is good soil drainage before using sulfur.

# SALT

In some soils, a salt build-up can create a serious problem for plants. The primary source of salt is irrigation water and turfgrasses vary in ability to tolerate high soil salt levels. This first symptom of a salt problem is reduced growth. As salt levels increase, a white salt deposit usually is seen on the soil surface. A soil test can determine soluble salt levels. While a few hundred parts per million (p.p.m.) won't do any apparent harm, most plants will die if levels reach 2,000 p.p.m.

The only way to reduce a soil salt problem is to improve internal soil drainage so that the salts are leached out of the root zone. This is accomplished by aerification (see Chapter 11) and/or through the use of a soil wetting agent.

# IV
## PLANTING METHODS

When putting in a new lawn, remember one thing: If it's done right the first time, it should never have to be done again. By making careful plans and following these 10 basic steps, you can have a thick green carpet that will be the envy of the whole neighborhood.

    **1. Remove rocks and other debris from your yard.** In fact, try to remove all objects that can cause problems later. For example, leftover construction debris, if buried, can cause drainage problems. Rocks or pieces of concrete can interfere with mowing. And buried organic material, such as pieces of lumber, will decay and cause an area of the lawn to sink.

    **2. Kill the weeds.** Many homesites have a severe weed problem that should be eliminated at the outset. Many annual weeds will be killed when the soil is tilled, but not perennial weeds like dallisgrass and Johnsongrass. It's very hard to control perennial weeds the first year of the new lawn. Therefore, the time to get rid of them is before the lawn is planted. Use a herbicide containing glyphosate. When applied properly, it kills the whole weed plant and not just the leaves.

    **3. Apply fertilizer.** The germinating grass seed, sprouting sprigs

The first step to establishing a good lawn is to clear it of rocks and debris (top). And the best time to kill weeds (bottom) is before a lawn is planted. This can be done with the proper application of a herbicide containing glyphosate.

**Table 4-1**
**FERTILIZER RATES**

| Fertilizer analysis | Pounds per 1,000 Sq. Ft. |
| --- | --- |
| 10-20-10 | 10 |
| 16-20-0 | 10 |
| 12-12-12 | 17 |
| 18-18-18 | 11 |
| 10-10-10 | 20 |

or sod growing new roots all benefit from a good supply of phosphorous in the soil. It is the key nutrient necessary in lawn establishment and should be applied at the rate indicated in one of the examples in Table 4-1. Phosphorous moves downward very slowly into the soil when applied to the surface. It must be worked into the soil so that it will reach the grass plants' roots.

**4. Till the soil.** There are several reasons why the soil should be tilled before planting seed, sod or sprigs. Seeds and sprigs should be slightly buried and pieces of sod must be in contact with the soil surface. A loose, finely tilled soil will make this possible. Till to a depth of 3 to 4 inches.

**5. Rake the lawn.** Rake the tilled soil and remove any rocks or debris that were brought to the surface when tilling. This raking should level the surface.

**6. Apply seed, sprigs or sod.** The method to use in establishing a lawn depends on the variety of the turfgrass you select and your budget. Sodding is the most expensive, followed by sprigging, plugging and seeding. The rate usually used to sprig a lawn is from 5 to 7 bushels per 1,000 square feet.

A bushel of sprigs is defined as 1 square yard of shredded sod. In this way, a square yard of sod can be made to establish more than 20 square yards of new lawn. Plugs usually are set on 12-inch centers. Seeding may be accomplished by using either hydromulching or hydroseeding. This usually means that a solution containing a fertilizer, seed and a mulch is applied evenly over the soil. The great advantage is that the new lawn will have fewer erosion problems and the initial watering will not be as critical. The mulch will act to conserve moisture and fewer waterings will be necessary to get the seed to germinate.

**A lawn should be tilled to a depth of 3 to 4 inches and then raked to clear it of rocks and debris before planting.**

**Applying sod is the most effective and the most expensive way to install a lawn.**

Seeding rates (Table 4-2) are approximate and the better job you do of preparing the soil, the better the chance that lower rates will be adequate. Here are some other factors to keep in mind when purchasing seed.

**Seed Quality:** On each box or bag of turfgrass seed there is a label that contains some information that will help in evaluating the quality of that seed. The important things to look for are:

**Purity:** This is the percentage of pure seed in the container. In the example shown in Figure 4-1, 93.66 percent of the material in the bag is buffalograss seed.

**Germination:** This means that 88 percent of the pure buffalograss seed in the bag will germinate. There is a term used, called ''Pure Live Seed'' or PLS. It is found by multiplying the purity (93.66 percent) by the germination (88 percent). The resulting 82 percent means that 82 percent of the material in the bag can establish

| Table: 4-2 | |
| :---: | :---: |
| Seeding Rates | |
| **Variety** | **Pounds per 1,000 Sq. Ft.** |
| Common Bermuda | 1-2 |
| Kentucky Bluegrass | 1-2 |
| Tall Fescue | 8-10 |
| Buffalograss* | 5 + |
| Centipede * | 2 + |

*The cost of seed makes price a bigger factor than the seeding rate.

buffalograss plants if it receives proper care. The higher the PLS number, the better the seed.

**Other Crop:** This term is used to indicate the presence of any other turfgrass seed.

**Inert:** This is simply trash and should be as low as possible.

**Weeds:** This also should be low and there should not be any noxious weeds.

**Test Date:** This should be fairly recent. Seed with an old test date may not be very good.

**Certified Seed:** There may be another label found on the seed container (Figure 4-2). It may be ''certified'' seed. The fact that it is certified has nothing at all to do with its quality in terms of purity or germination. The term ''certified'' means that an independent agency, such as a state university or Department of Agriculture, has examined the fields and has determined it is indeed the particular variety of turfgrass indicated on the label. In the example label, Oregon State University has certified that the seed in the bag is Galway tall fescue. Buying certified seed is the only sure way to know the variety of a turfgrass in the container is what it says it is.

**7. Make final raking and rolling.** If you plant seed, lightly rake the seed bed to move the seed just under the soil's surface. No matter what type grass you use or how it's planted, the next-to-last step in installing a lawn is a light rolling. This helps firm the soil and puts the seed or sprig in good contact with the soil. Rolling helps eliminate any air pockets that might be present under the sod.

**8. Water lightly and often.** The newly seeded or sprigged lawn should be kept moist, not saturated. Frequent, light waterings are

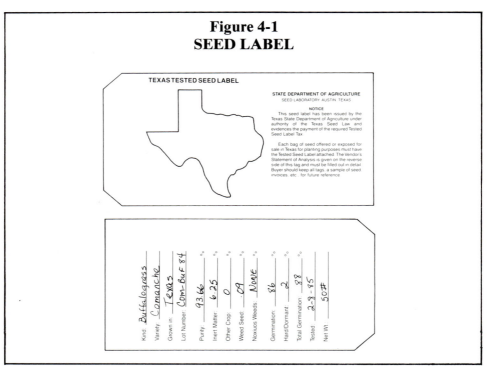

Figure 4-1
SEED LABEL

Figure 4-2
CERTIFIED SEED LABEL

**The next-to-last step in installing any lawn is a light rolling to make sure the lawn will be level.**

necessary for good germination. This may mean watering three or four times a day. (If you've hydromulched or hydrosprigged, this many waterings a day may not be necessary.) This regime should continue until the young grass plants are visible. Then the frequency of watering should be reduced. After four to six weeks, the waterings should become fairly infrequent and the new lawn should be treated the same as an established one.

If you plant sod, it should be soaked completely each time it's watered and should be watered again when it dries out. In about two weeks, the roots should be developed enough so that you should be able to water at fairly infrequent intervals as with an established lawn.

**9. Mowing.** Generally, the more often a new lawn is mowed, the faster it will spread and form a thick, dense turf that resists weed invasion.

**10. Continue weed control.** Generally, weed control using chemicals should be avoided until the lawn is fairly well-established,

If a newly planted bermuda lawn gets too wet, the grass plants will turn purple. Cutting back on watering usually will solve the problem.

which usually takes about six to eight weeks for seed or sprigged lawns. Sodded lawns are much faster. Annual weeds, which probably are the biggest weed problem, usually are controlled by mowing. If possible, avoid the use of MSMA or DSMA for the first growing season.

# PROBLEMS

It should be reasonably easy to start a lawn regardless of the turfgrass variety used but there can be problems. Here are a few of the most common ones to watch for:

**1. Not enough water.** This is common with lawns seeded during the hot, dry summer. They must be kept moist and not allowed to dry out in the first few weeks.

**2. Too much water.** This usually happens during rainier times of the year and may cause diseases to develop. Common bermuda that is

**A bermudagrass lawn ready for its first mowing.**

over-watered turns a purple or reddish-purple and the soil may erode. Simply reduce watering to cure either problem.

    **3. Over-watered and over-fertilized.** These lawns develop a very shallow root system and may not make it through the first winter.

    **4. Perennial weeds.** These weeds can give the new grass plants some serious competition. This is a direct result of not taking measures to control weeds before planting your grass.

# V
## MOWING

**P**erhaps the single most important cultural practice associated with maintaining any turfgrass is mowing. When considering the effects that mowing can have on your grass, you should remember that grass plants are designed by nature to grow and mature to a much taller height than they are maintained at by mowing. Mowing, in a sense, is not normal because it tends to upset the natural growth patterns of the plant.

## UNDERSTANDING YOUR GRASS

To provide a quality turf, you must understand a little bit about how the turfgrass plant operates. The first, or at least the most apparent, effect of mowing is the reduction of the plant's leaf surface area. The leaf system manufactures and supplies the plant with carbohydrates, which is analogous to the food we eat. During the active growing months (spring and fall for the cool-season grasses and in the summer for warm-season grasses), carbohydrate production is high and the plant is able to store food reserves. During periods of stress or dormancy, the plant must draw on these reserves to survive.

If you mow too low during periods that are favorable to

| Table 5-1 MOWER SETTINGS AND WHEN TO MOW (In Inches) | | |
|---|---|---|
| **Variety** | **Mower Setting** | **Height Of Grass Before Mowing** |
| Common Bermuda | 1½ | 2¼ |
| Hybrid Bermuda | 1 | 1½ |
| St. Augustine | 2 | 3 |
| Tall Fescue | 2½ | 3½ |
| Centipede | 2 | 3 |
| Zoysia | 2 | 3 |
| Buffalograss | 2 | 3 |
| Kentucky Bluegrass | 2 | 3 |
| Winter Lawn | 2 | 3 |

carbohydrate storage, you may seriously impair the plant's ability to develop adequate food reserves for stress or dormant periods. The resulting death of the plant may be falsely attributed to heat or cold injury when, in fact, the food reserves simply were not sufficient to carry it through the stress period.

When part of the plant's leaves are removed by mowing, it reacts by increasing leaf growth to re-establish its former leaf surface area. This flush of leaf growth requires carbohydrates and may reduce the supply of carbohydrates available to the root system. In the "pecking order" of the plant, the leaf system has priority over roots, rhizomes or stolons for carbohydrates. Thus, the demand for carbohydrates by the leaves after mowing may result in the reduction of root growth. The greater percentage of leaf tissue removed, the longer root growth may be reduced. This is one reason why it is strongly recommended that no more than one-third of the leaf surface be removed at any one mowing. (See Table 5-1 for information on when to mow.)

The cutting height also has an effect on root growth. There is a direct relationship between cutting height and the total volume of root system. The turfgrass plant, just like all other plants, develops a balance between its top parts and its root system. A certain size of root system is needed to support a certain volume of top growth and vice versa. If either the top parts or the root system is reduced, the plant will react by reducing the other. Think about transplanting a tree. The top is pruned to compensate for the root system that is lost in the digging operation. When we mow the turfgrass plant we are reducing its top parts. The

**Mowing a lawn is considered by many to be the most time-consuming and unpleasant lawn-maintenance task, but the job will be easier if you take good care of the lawn.**

plant no longer needs the same size root system and reduces it to achieve balance. The more we reduce its top growth (i.e. the lower the cutting height), the shallower the root system may become, which may seriously impair the plant's ability to withstand stress, especially drought stress.

The leaf system has another important function—insulation. The growing points, or crowns, of most turfgrass plants are at or near the surface of the soil and are very high in the chemical activities that control the growth processes. These growing points are very temperature sensitive. The upper optimum temperature range for cool-season turfgrasses is about 75 degrees and about 85 degrees for warm-season turfgrasses. When the temperature at the growing point goes above these temperatures, the growth process begins to slow down. If the temperature at the growing point gets too high for a long enough period, especially with cool-season grasses, the plant goes into what we call summer dormancy.

**Generally, it's best to leave your grass clippings on the lawn to serve as a mulch. But if you let your grass get too high between mowings, as in the photo above, there will be too many clippings to decompose properly and you'll need to rake them.**

However, the leaf surface insulates the growing point from high temperatures. Thus, when we reduce the leaf surface area, we also reduce the amount of insulation available for the growing point. If you cut your grass too low, it will be more susceptible to high temperature injury.

Most of the turfgrasses are subjected to some degree of wear. Golf course putting greens and athletic fields generally receive some of the highest wear of any turf area, as do some home lawns. The leaf surface area protects the growing point of the plant from direct mechanical injury associated with traffic. As the leaf surface is reduced, the overall wearability of the turf is reduced. Turfs cut at low heights are subject to high-wear damage and tend to thin out gradually.

Mowing practices may have an effect on the incidence of disease, with diseases being more common among plants that are weaker because of being cut too low.

Just as the proper selection of height-of-cut is important, so is the frequency at which the turf is mowed. Ideally, the time between mowings should be as long as possible to allow the plant to recover from the last cutting. Leaf growth rate and the intended use of the turf will, to a large degree, dictate the mowing frequency.

If you apply high rates of nitrogen to your lawn, you may be forced to increase the frequency of mowings. This is especially true when the high rates of nitrogen are supplied in a soluble form. If because of high growth rates you have to mow your lawn too frequently, you should consider adjusting both nitrogen rate and source. The slower-releasing nitrogen materials do not tend to produce the lush growth associated with the soluble sources and should allow a longer period between mowings.

In most situations, grass clippings are not removed after mowing. Removal may be required, though, when the clippings interfere with the intended use of the turf (i.e. the golf course putting green) or when they are too heavy and tend to smother the turf. Generally, the shorter the clippings the better they tend to fall deep into the turf and the more rapid their decomposition. Clippings do not contribute to thatch so there is no need to ''bag'' them if a reasonable mowing program is followed.

Mowing practices are extremely important in any turfgrass management program. The proper selection of height-of-cut, the proper mowing frequency, the use of a mower with a sharp blade, and the development of a reasonable growth rate can have a profound effect on the health and vigor of any turfgrass system.

# COMPOSTING

If for any reason grass clippings must be bagged, it's a good idea to use them in a compost pile, which is excellent for improving soil.

Composting is the natural decomposition of organic matter, such as grass clippings, dry leaves, sawdust, gin trash, sod, hay or weeds. Kitchen scraps may be used but don't use grease, fat or meat trimmings because they break down slowly, attract rodents and pests, and produce an unpleasant odor. Composting grass clippings and other plant materials eliminates the cost of bagging, collecting and disposing of them. Compost adds nutrients to the soil, improves its physical characteristics and its ability to hold water and nutrients. Compost can

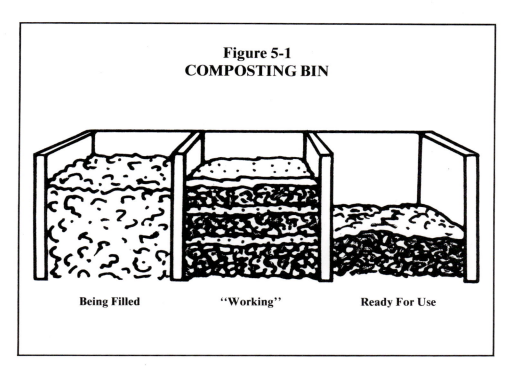

**Figure 5-1**
**COMPOSTING BIN**

**Being Filled**          **"Working"**          **Ready For Use**

be used as a mulch around vegetables, shrubs and flowers or can be
worked into the soil to add nutrients and improve soil quality.

If prepared properly, compost reaches about 160 degrees or
more, which destroys most weed seeds, insects and disease organisms.
Composting requires organic materials, micro-organisms, air, water
and a small amount of nitrogen fertilizer. A small amount of garden soil
or manure provides sufficient micro-organisms to break down the
organic material. Too much nitrogen will kill the microbes and too
much water causes insufficient air and hinders composting.

The compost pile can be freestanding, but requires less room if it
is enclosed. Wire fencing, cement blocks, bricks or scrap lumber make
good enclosures. Leave one side open so the compost can be turned with
a fork and so air can enter the pile. For best results, the pile should be at
least 4 feet across and 5 feet tall after settling. If space is available, make
three piles to have one ready for use, one being filled and one
"working." If space is limited, two piles are better than one, but one
will work. About 90 to 120 days are required to prepare good compost.
(See Figure 5-1.)

# LAWN MOWER SELECTION

Price, as with most things we buy, seems to have a great influence on our selection of a lawn mower. And while there is no question about the importance of price, there are other considerations that also should play a part in the selection of a lawn mower.

In general, the upper cutting height limit for a reel-type mower is about 2 inches. The lower cutting height limit for a rotary-type mower is about 1 inch. As indicated in Table 5-2, the variety of turfgrass in the lawn should be considered in the selection of mower type.

Most turfgrass experts suggest that a reel-type mower has a superior cutting action to that of a rotary. The scissor-like cutting action of the reel type tends to produce a cleaner cut on the leaf blade. If a rotary mower's blade is kept sharp, it also will produce a clean cut. If you select a rotary mower, it might be wise to pick up an extra blade so that you can replace the dull blade with a sharp one every month or so. This gives you a whole month to get the blade sharpened before it is due to go back on the mower.

Some lawn mowers are advertised as mulching mowers. The idea is that they will cut up the leaf blades and other lawn debris into smaller pieces so that they will decompose faster. This probably is true, but if the lawn is cut so that no more than a third of the leaf blade is removed at any one mowing, the resulting clippings are usually small enough so that they will decompose fairly rapidly and not contribute to any thatch. If you tend to let your grass get too long between mowings, a mulching mower may be of benefit. It's better for the lawn, though, to mow more frequently than to let it get too high and have to rely on the mulching action of a mower.

You should determine if the engine of the gas power mower you

| Table 5-2 TURFGRASS VARIETY AND MOWER SELECTION | | |
|---|---|---|
| **Turfgrass** | **Cutting Height** | **Mower Type** |
| Common Bermudagrass | 1½ inches | Reel or Rotary |
| Hybrid (Tif) Bermudagrass | 1 inch | Reel |
| St. Augustinegrass | 2 inches | Reel or Rotary |
| Tall Fescue | 2½ inches | Rotary |
| Bluegrass | 2 inches | Reel or Rotary |

The cutting action of a reel mower is shown above. If a mower's blades get dull, the blades of grass will look ragged (bottom).

| Table 5-3 NUMBER OF BLADES NEEDED FOR INTENDED CUTTING HEIGHT | |
| --- | --- |
| **Intended Cutting Height** | **Number of Blades on Reel** |
| below ½ inch | 7 or 8 |
| between 1 and ½ inch | 6 |
| above 1 inch | 5 |

are considering is either two or four cycle. A two-cycle engine burns a gas-oil mixture while a four-cycle engine uses straight gasoline. A four-cycle engine requires an oil change at certain intervals while a two-cycle does not.

Some other considerations in selecting a mower are ease of mowing height selection adjustment, ease of blade removal and replacement (rotary), ease of oil changing if it is a four-cycle engine, and the location of the controls. Also, you might consider who you are buying the mower from—you may need some service later on and you want to be sure it can be provided. If a reel-type mower is selected, the number of blades on the reel and the intended height of cut should be considered. (See Table 5-3.)

# SCALPING

Each spring, many homeowners go through a process of removing the dead grass from their lawns. This process has been called "scalping" or, more incorrectly, "de-thatching." Thatch is a layer of organic material that under certain conditions may develop between the base, or crown, of the plant and the soil surface. Scalping involves the removal of the dead upper parts of the plant.

Another reason why scalped lawns "turn" green earlier is that just the physical removal of all the brown material may allow more of the green to be visible at first.

Scalping a turf in the spring is not a part of any professional turf management program. Athletic fields, golf courses and similar areas are maintained without scalping. Most homeowners consider scalping to be a very dirty, unpleasant job, which for an average size city generates hundreds and thousands of bags of grass material. All these bags find their way to our area landfills where space is already at a premium.

Many cities must pay overtime in the spring just to deal with this tremendous volume of dead grass and, of course, the irony of the situation is that this is all unnecessary. Scalping is not necessary to produce a good quality lawn. Proper mowing techniques, the timely use of the right fertilizer and the timely application of water go together to produce a quality lawn.

# VI
## IRRIGATING

Watering is one of the most basic practices in maintaining a home lawn. You only have to experience one of Texas' summer droughts to appreciate the need for periodic watering. Like most of our landscape plants, the turfgrasses, with the possible exception of buffalograss, may not survive a dry summer without the judicious application of water.

Plants vary in their expression of drought stress. The leaves of some plants begin to droop. Other plants, such as the turfgrasses, dry up and the leaves roll and turn a dull, purplish color.

### TOO MUCH WATER, TOO BAD

Just as the *lack* of water has a deleterious effect on plants, so does *too much* water. The root system of a plant must take in oxygen and give off carbon dioxide to live. When water is applied too frequently, the soil becomes saturated and the movement of oxygen into the soil and the movement of carbon dioxide out of the soil is stopped. The net result is a condition in the plant termed ''wet wilt'' and, if not corrected, the plant will die quickly.

There are many ways you can water your lawn, including with a travelling sprinkler as shown above. No matter what system you use, it's important to keep your soil adequately moist.

**Table 6-1**
**THE RELATIVE NEED OF TURFGRASSES FOR WATER**

1. Buffalograss (requires the least)
2. Common Bermuda
3. Zoysia
4. "Tif" Bermuda
5. St. Augustine
6. Centipede
7. Bluegrass
8. Tall Fescue (requires the most)

Many of our soils are high in clay and tend to shrink when they are dry. It is not uncommon to see large cracks develop in lawns during the summer. While the development of these cracks usually does not cause serious damage to the turfgrass plant, they certainly can pose a safety hazard for those using the lawn as a play area. Also, if houses are built on these soils and the soil is allowed to dry to the point of cracking, the foundation of the house also may crack. The timely application of water will prevent these problems.

The amount of water needed varies greatly among turfgrasses, and consideration of this fact when establishing a lawn may significantly reduce the need for irrigation during the summer. (See Table 6-1.)

# NEW LAWNS

Newly seeded or sprigged lawns should be watered lightly at frequent intervals. The seed, or sprigs, must be kept moist but not saturated during this initial growth period. This may well mean that an application of water might be necessary as many as four or five times on hot, windy days. The first 10 to 14 days is especially critical. If these young plants are allowed to dry out, they may die. After about two weeks, the development of root systems should be well underway and the watering frequency should be reduced slowly. About one month after seeding or sprigging, the new lawn should be treated as an established lawn. Purple or red seedling bermudagrass may be a symptom that it is being over-watered. If this occurs, reduce watering and the plants usually recover on their own.

Newly sodded lawns should be watered much like established lawns, except more frequently. After the sod is applied, it should be soaked with enough water so that the soil under the sod is wet to a depth of 2 or 3 inches. Each time the sod begins to dry out, it should be re-soaked. Roots develop fairly rapidly and within two weeks or so it should be ready to be treated like an established lawn.

# ESTABLISHED LAWNS: WHEN TO WATER

Ideally, a lawn should be watered just before it begins to wilt. Most grasses take on a dull purplish cast and the leaf blades begin to fold or roll. Grass under drought stress also shows evidence of tracks after someone walks across the lawn. These are the first signs of wilt. With some careful observation and experience, it shouldn't be too hard to determine just how many days a lawn can go between waterings. Common bermudagrass lawns should be able to go five to seven days or even longer between waterings without loss of quality.

Early morning is considered the best time to water. The wind usually is calm and the temperature is low so less water is lost to evaporation. The worst time to water is in late evening because the lawn tends to stay wet all night, making it more susceptible to disease. The quicker the grass plant dries off after irrigation, the better off it is.

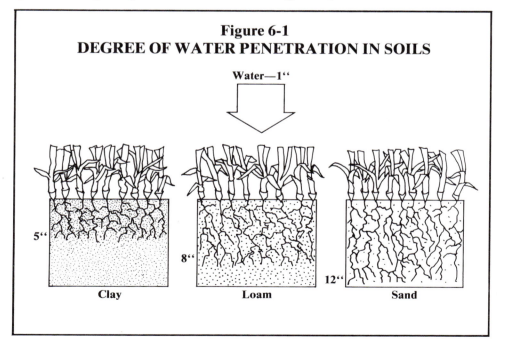

**Figure 6-1**
**DEGREE OF WATER PENETRATION IN SOILS**

Water—1"

Clay    Loam    Sand

5"    8"    12"

# HOW MUCH WATER

When a lawn needs to be watered, enough should be applied so that the soil is wet to a depth of 4 to 6 inches. The type of soil has a great deal to do with how much water is needed to wet soil to the desired depth. In Figure 6-1, note the depth of wetting resulting from the application of 1 inch of water. According to this, it should take about ½ inch of water to achieve the desired wetting depth if the soil is high in sand, and about ¾ inch of water if the soil is a loam. For soils high in clay, an inch of water usually is necessary to wet the soil to the desired depth.

If the water application rates are too light or too frequent, the lawn may tend to become weak and shallow rooted, which in turn makes it more susceptible to stress injury. (See Figure 6-2.)

# HOW TO WATER

The following steps will allow you to find out how much water your sprinkler or sprinkler system puts out and to check its distribution pattern at the same time.

1. Determine the rate at which your sprinkler applies water to the lawn.

    A. Set out three to five empty cans in a straight line going away from sprinkler. (See Figure 6-3.) Set the last can near the edge of the sprinkler's coverage.

    B. Run the sprinkler for a set period of time, such as one-half hour.

    C. Measure the amount of water in each can.

    D. If runoff occurs, repeat steps A, B and C until at least 1 inch water been applied and allowed to soak into the soil.

2. Run sprinkler or sprinkler system long enough to apply at least 1 inch of water or until runoff occurs. If runoff occurs first, take these steps:

    A. Stop sprinkler and note running time.

    B. Allow water to soak in for half an hour or longer.

    C. Start sprinkler.

    D. If runoff occurs, repeat steps A, B and C until at least 1 inch of water has been applied and allowed to soak into the soil.

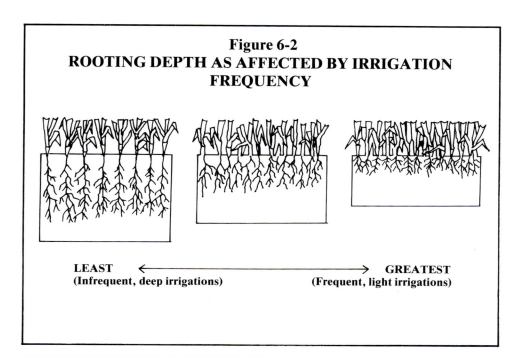

**Figure 6-2**
**ROOTING DEPTH AS AFFECTED BY IRRIGATION FREQUENCY**

LEAST
(Infrequent, deep irrigations)

GREATEST
(Frequent, light irrigations)

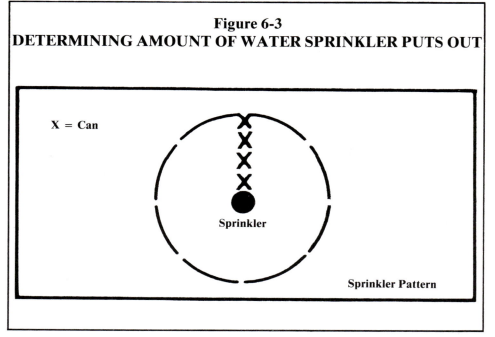

**Figure 6-3**
**DETERMINING AMOUNT OF WATER SPRINKLER PUTS OUT**

X = Can

Sprinkler

Sprinkler Pattern

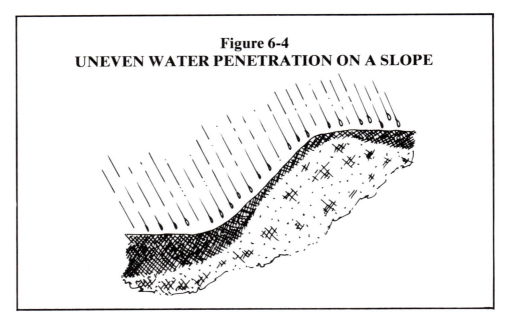

**Figure 6-4**
**UNEVEN WATER PENETRATION ON A SLOPE**

3. Do not water again until the lawn has completely dried out. (This usually means five or six days).

# OTHER FACTORS TO CONSIDER

**Soil Type:** Water penetrates a sandy soil much faster than a clay soil, so lawns grown on sandy soils will require more frequent watering than those grown on soils that are high in clay. Because water moves fairly slowly into a clay soil, the rate at which water is applied to this type of lawn should be as slow as possible.

**Slope:** Lawns with a high degree of slope present a particular problem. It is very easy for water to run down the slope without penetrating the soil. Water must be applied at very slow rates from sprinklers near the top of the slope. Sprinklers on the slope or near the bottom of the slope may prove ineffective. (See Figure 6-4.)

**Fertilizer:** The faster the lawn grows, the more water it requires. The slow-release fertilizers that contain materials like sulfur-coated urea or ureaformaldehyde as nitrogen sources do not tend to produce high growth rates. Heavy applications of fertilizers high in soluble nitrogen should be avoided.

If not watered properly, your grass can wilt as shown in the tall fescue lawn at top. But be careful when watering your lawn not to also water the street. Keep in mind, though, that water running off the lawn doesn't necessarily mean your soil is watered adequately.

**Management Factors:** The use of an aerifier or coring device will aid in increasing movement of water into the soil. A surfactant, or wetting agent, also may aid the movement of water into high clay soils.

# SUMMARY

1. Apply enough water to wet the soil to a depth of 4 to 6 inches.
2. Avoid frequent light applications of water.
3. Water in the early daylight hours.
4. Select a turfgrass that has a low water requirement.
5. Avoid using high rates of soluble nitrogen fertilizers. (They tend to promote high growth rates which, in turn, increase the water requirements of the plant.)

# IRRIGATION SYSTEMS

All the water in the world can't help a lawn if it is not applied efficiently. There is a great array of both aboveground and below-ground irrigation equipment available for home lawn use. In making a choice, there are a number of facts that should be considered:

**Application Pattern:** It doesn't make too much sense to use a sprinkler that produces a square or rectangular pattern when the lawn has a basically round shape. In-ground systems are designed to fit the shape of the lawn. If aboveground sprinklers are used, care must be taken in their selection to make sure it provides an even pattern of water, regardless of whether it has a round or square shape. Typically, these sprinklers must be moved around the lawn, which may have an effect on just how evenly the whole lawn gets watered. Generally, the chances are better of getting a good, even application of water on the lawn when a well-designed, in-ground sprinkler system is used—unless the operator of the aboveground system has taken great care in the selection of the hose and sprinkler and in its operation.

**Droplet Size:** Regardless of the type of system selected, the size of water droplet the sprinkler head produces is important. The finer the droplet size, the easier it is for the designed pattern of that sprinkler head to become distorted by wind. In many areas, it may be a rare day when the wind doesn't blow. Large droplets are not as easily distorted as small ones by the wind. Another problem associated with a system that produces fine water droplets is the fact that small droplets are more subject to evaporation than large droplets.

**Operation Ease:** An in-ground system with an automatic timer probably is by far the easiest to use. Since the best time to water is in the early morning, that fact alone might help one select an automatic system.

**How To Buy A System:** There are a lot of people out there selling irrigation systems. The best way to check on your prospective installer is to ask for and check on references. The newer systems, to a large degree, will only be as good as the company that installs them.

# VII
## FERTILIZING

A good reasonable fertilizer program is one of the basic parts of any turfgrass maintenance program. Lawns that are under-fertilized tend to be thin and have poor color while lawns that are over-fertilized, especially with high levels of a soluble nitrogen fertilizer, may tend to develop excessive thatch and be more prone to insect and disease damage.

### REQUIRED NUTRIENTS

All plants require some 15 or 16 different nutrients for their growth. The soil, in most cases, is a vast reservoir of these plant nutrients, but soils vary in the amount of nutrients they contain and in their ability to get those nutrients to plants. When a plant requires more of a nutrient than the soil can supply, or requires a nutrient not present in the soil, then a fertilizer must be used. A soil test can measure the nutrients that are present.

Of all the nutrients required by the turfgrass plant, three— nitrogen (N), phosphorus (P) and potasium (K)—usually are not available in the soil in high enough quantities for good growth and must be added periodically as a fertilizer. In some special situations, such as

**Proper applications of fertilizer can help your lawn be thick and green.**

when soils are highly acid or alkaline, other nutrients like iron or magnesium may be required.

# NITROGEN

The turfgrass plant requires more nitrogen than any of the other plant nutrients. It's not uncommon for the levels of nitrogen in the plant to be as much as 4 or 5 percent. Nitrogen is a part of chlorophyll and has a great deal to do with nearly all the growth and development phases in the plant.

As the amount of nitrogen supplied to the plant increases, the rate of shoot, or leaf growth, increases. This increase generally is at the expense of root growth. Rapid leaf growth tends to use up all the food material being produced by the plant and very little is left for the roots and other organs, such as stolons or runners. It is very possible to produce a lawn with very high leaf growth and a good green color, but with a very restricted root system. This is one reason why minimal levels of nitrogen usually are desirable.

High levels of nitrogen tend to produce a plant that has thin cell walls and a high water percentage in its tissue. The thickness of a cell wall may be very important when a fungus or any insect is trying to invade the plant. A plant that contains a high percentage of water requires more irrigation and is more susceptible to heat and drought stress.

The amount of nitrogen supplied to the turf plant has a great deal to do with the amount of food reserve the plant is able to store for periods of unfavorable weather, such as the period termed "winter dormancy." The plant manufactures food material, called carbohydrates, in the leaf tissue. Since the leaves have priority over the other plant parts for growth and since nitrogen stimulates leaf growth, the oversupply of nitrogen may promote leaf growth to the point of using up all the food material the plant can supply, especially during the fall of the year. If this happens, little food material is available for storage and the plant may not live through the winter. The goal of a good fertility program should be to produce dark green top growth and high root growth.

# PHOSPHORUS

For years, many text books have suggested that phosphorus was necessary for root growth. This is true, but only in the sense that some amount of nutrients are needed for the optimum growth of all parts of the plant. Phosphorus is important to the processes of transferring and storing energy within the plant. Thus, since roots are a primary organ for energy storage, they have a dependency on phosphorus. The formation and germination of the seed also creates a high demand for phosphorus. A high level of energy must be stored in the seed so that it can survive until it can germinate.

Since turf plants usually are not maintained for their seed production their need for phosphorus is rather low, which should be reflected in the type of fertilizer used. The exception to this rule, however, is that a fertilizer containing higher levels of phosphorus is suggested when a turf is to be established from seed, sod or sprigs. Phosphorus is an element that moves very slowly in the soil, so slowly that it may take years to move just a few inches. Of course, the speed of movement depends on the amount of clay in the soil: the higher the clay content, the slower the phosphorus moves. This movement, combined with the relatively high demand of phosphorus when you first establish a lawn, makes it highly desirable to incorporate a fertilizer with a N-P-K ratio of 1-1-1 or 1-2-2 in the soil before planting.

# POTASSIUM

Many plant growth experts consider potassium to be the plant nutrient that has been passed over and not given proper credit for the role it plays in plant growth. Part of the problem is that the way potassium functions is not well-understood, while the functions of other nutrients, such as nitrogen and phosphorus, have been more clearly defined. Potassium seems to be involved in many growth processes, but its most important role has to do with water relations within the plant.

The absence of adequate amounts of potassium tends to produce a plant with thin cell walls and a high water content, the same characteristics produced by high levels of nitrogen. As the amount of potassium supplied to the plant is increased in relationship to the level of nitrogen, cell walls are thicker and the water content of the plant drops. This makes the plant more stress tolerant and less susceptible to invasion of a disease or an insect attack.

Potassium has a great deal to do with the balance in the plant between leaf and root growth. As the level of potassium supplied to the plant is increased in relationship to the level of nitrogen, the rate of leaf growth tends to be reduced. With this reduced demand for food material by the leaves, more food then becomes available for stolon, rhizome and root growth.

Potassium is considered to be the most leachable of the plant

| Table 7-1 EXAMPLES OF FERTILIZER ANALYSIS | | | |
|---|---|---|---|
| **Fertilizer Ratios**  1-1-1 | 1-2-2 | 3-1-2 | 4-1-2 |
| **Fertilizer Analysis**  8-8-8 12-12-12 etc. | 5-10-10 10-20-20 etc. | 15-5-10 12-4-8 etc. | 16-4-8 20-5-10 etc. |

nutrients and must be supplied at a rather constant rate. It may even be lost from the plant through its leaves during a rain or when watering.

The use of fertilizers with relatively high levels of potassium has been hard to "sell" because, unlike other nutrients, its use does not necessarily result in a change that is easy to measure. Research has shown, however, that when potassium is supplied in optimum levels, the turf plant is less susceptible to such factors as drought, heat, cold and disease.

# FERTILIZER RATIOS AND ANALYSIS

There are several factors that are used when considering the best ratio between nitrogen, phosphorus and potassium for a turf fertilizer. Considered are the functions of each nutrient in the plant, the amount of each nutrient required by the plant and the relationship between each nutrient in the growth of the the plant.

Putting these factors all together, research has shown that the best N-P-K ratio for turf establishment is 1-1-1 or 1-2-2. For a mature established turf, the best N-P-K ratio seems to be 3-1-2 or 4-1-2. Table 7-1 defines examples of fertilizer analysis that fit the suggested rates.

# YEARLY FERTILIZER NEEDED

The grasses used for lawns vary in the amount of fertilizer they need for optimum growth during the year. (See Table 7-2.) Because of the wide variety of fertilizer ratios available, application rates usually are expressed as pounds of nitrogen (the first number in the analysis) per 1,000 square feet.

# APPLICATION RATE AND TIMING

Both the rate at which a fertilizer is applied to a lawn and the interval between applications have a great deal to do with the form of nitrogen used in the fertilizer. (See Table 7-3.) It generally is recommended that a quickly available nitrogen fertilizer not be applied at a rate any greater than 1 pound of actual nitrogen per 1,000 square feet per application. To find out how much of a given fertilizer it takes to have a pound of nitrogen, simply divide the first number of the analysis (the percentage of nitrogen) into 100. For example, if the fertilizer has a 15-5-10 analysis, 15 goes into 100 about seven times, so 7 pounds of 15-5-10 contains 1 pound of nitrogen. The slowly available

**Table 7-2**
**FERTILIZER REQUIREMENTS**

| Turfgrass | Pounds of Nitrogen per 1,000 sq. ft. per year |
|---|---|
| Hybrid bermudagrass (Tifway, Tifgreen) | 5 - 7 |
| Common bermudagrass | 4 - 6 |
| Bluegrass | 4 -6 |
| Zoysiagrass | 3 - 5 |
| St. Augustinegrass | 2 - 4 |
| Tall Fescue | 2 - 4 |
| Centipedegrass | 1 - 2 |
| Buffalograss | 1 |

**Table 7-3**
**FORMS OF NITROGEN**

| Quickly Available | Slowly Available |
|---|---|
| urea | ureaformaldehyde (UF) |
| ammonium sulfate | sulfur-coated urea (SCU) |
| ammonium nitrate | isobutylidine diurea (IBDU) |

material may be applied at higher rates. The relative difference in growth rates that result from the same amount of nitrogen as a function of the form of nitrogen is illustrated in Figure 7-1.

Lawns should not be fertilized during periods of dormancy or during stress periods. Dormancy occurs during the winter for the warm-season grasses such as bermudagrass, St. Augustinegrass, buffalograss and centipedegrass. The first application of fertilizer on these lawns should be made in the spring after they have "greened up." The last application should be made in North Texas around September 1 and around October 1 in the southern part of the state.

A slowly soluble fertilizer should be used on St. Augustinegrass during the summer months to reduce the chance of disease or insect damage. St. Augustinegrass may, from time to time, suffer from iron

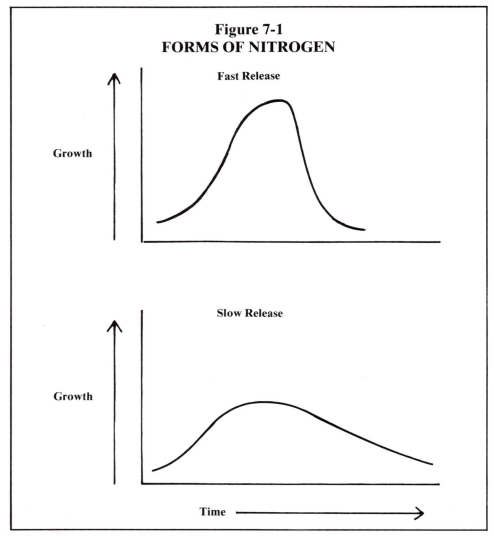

**Figure 7-1**
**FORMS OF NITROGEN**

chlorosis. Applications of iron sulfate or an iron chelate at the manufacturer's direction should eliminate the problem.

The cool-season grasses, such as tall fescue and bluegrass, should be fertilized during their active growth periods in the spring and fall, but not during periods when they are under stress, such as during hot weather.

# METHODS OF APPLICATION

A fertilizer can be applied effectively with either a "cyclone" type spreader or a drop-type spreader. Dark and light stripes may appear in the lawn as a result of an uneven fertilizer application. The best way to prevent this problem is to divide the total amount of fertilizer needed for the lawn into two equal amounts. Apply one-half of the total, using either type of spreader, in one direction and the rest at right angles to the first application. (See Figures 7-2 and 7-3.)

# WHY A FERTILIZER BURNS

One of the characteristics of soluble nitrogen fertilizer sources is their potential for "burning" turfgrasses. The risk of fertilizer burn is one of the reasons why there has been a tendency to use nitrogen fertilizers that contain a high percentage of slowly soluble nitrogen instead of totally soluble nitrogen fertilizers.

Soluble nitrogen fertilizers, if applied properly, can be just as effective as a slowly soluble fertilizer in providing the turfgrass plant with the nitrogen it requires. The risk of burn can be minimized if you understand the factors that contribute to a burn.

Fertilizers are salts. These salts are not unlike table salt except that they contain various plant nutrients. When a salt is added to water, the osmotic pressure of the solution is increased. Osmotic pressure is, in a sense, a measure of how tightly water is held in a solution. When a fertilizer, either as a solid or liquid, is applied to the surface of the soil, the salts must eventually enter and become a part of the soil solution—before the nutrients can enter the roots and be used by the turfgrass plant. The increase in the osmotic pressure of the soil solution associated with the application of a fertilizer may determine whether the plant will survive or will die from a fertilizer burn.

For a plant's root system to take in water, the water must pass through a root cell membrane. Water can pass through this membrane only when the osmotic pressure of the solution inside the cell is higher than the osmotic pressure of the soil solution outside the cell. Water moves from a solution with low osmotic pressure into a solution with higher osmotic pressure. If the osmotic pressure of the soil solution becomes higher than that of the solution inside the cell, water cannot enter the cell and may even move out of it. This results in the death of

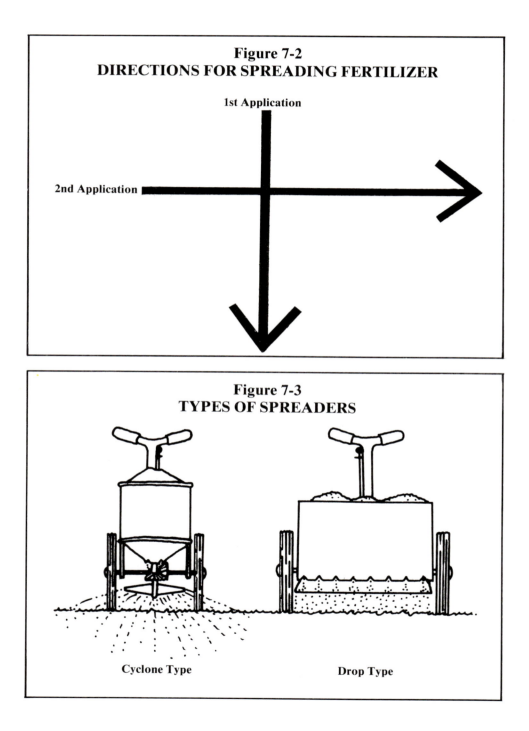

**Figure 7-2**
**DIRECTIONS FOR SPREADING FERTILIZER**

1st Application

2nd Application

**Figure 7-3**
**TYPES OF SPREADERS**

Cyclone Type                    Drop Type

the cell. When root cells die, the whole plant may die. The end result is termed a "fertilizer burn."

An understanding of the potential salt effect of the various fertilizer materials can help prevent possible fertilizer burn. Salt index values are a measure of a material's relative tendency to increase the osmotic pressure of the soil solution as compared with the increase caused by an equal weight of sodium nitrate. The salt index of sodium nitrate is 100. The higher the salt index, the greater the potential of material to increase the osmotic pressure of the soil solution and thus the potential for burn. As indicated in Tables 7-4 and 7-5, there are wide differences in the salt indexes of those fertilizer materials used.

Note that Table 7-4 also lists the salt indexes of selected nitrogen fertilizers in terms of single units of nitrogen. Nitrogen is applied on a unit basis (i.e.,per 1,000 square feet). Although a material such as ammonium sulfate has a lower salt index than urea, the salt effect of applied urea is lower because it contains a higher percentage of nitrogen.

The potential for burn does not depend totally on the salt index of the fertilizer material. The moisture status of the soil and of the turfgrass plant is also important. If the level of the soil solutions is low, a fertilizer will have a greater effect on increasing the osmotic pressure of the soil solution. When a fertilizer is "watered in," the volume of the soil solution increases and thus the osmotic pressure of the soil solution is reduced. In well-drained soils, however, heavy applications of water, while having the beneficial effect of reducing the osmotic pressure of the soil solution may also have the harmful effect of leaching nutrients past the root system.

The water status of the plant is affected by both the air temperature and the humidity, which is the amount of water in the air surrounding the plant. These factors to a large degree affect the plant's water requirements. As the air temperature increases, the plant requires more water and as the humidity decreases the plant requires more water. As the osmotic pressure of the soil solution increases, less and less water is available to the plant. Watering in a fertilizer material may increase the water available to the root system by decreasing the osmotic pressure of the soil solution, but may also aid in reducing the plant's water requirements by cooling the plant and increasing the humidity of the

**Table 7-4**
**SALT INDEX VALUES FOR COMMONLY USED NITROGEN FERTILIZER MATERIALS**

| Material | Approx. %N | Salt Index | Salt Index per Unit of N |
|---|---|---|---|
| Ammonium Nitrate | 33 | 105 | 3.2 |
| Ammonium Sulfate | 21 | 69 | 3.3 |
| Calcium Nitrate | 12 | 53 | 4.4 |
| I.B.D.U. | 31 | 5 | 0.1* |
| Potassium Nitrate | 14 | 74 | 5.3 |
| Natural Organic | 5 | 4 | 0.8 |
| UF | 38 | 10 | 0.3* |
| Urea | 45 | 75 | 1.7 |

*Sulfur-coated urea also has a low salt index—about these same values.

**Table 7-5**
**SALT INDEX VALUES FOR OTHER COMMONLY USED MATERIALS**

| Material | Approx. Nutrient Level | Salt Index |
|---|---|---|
| Superphosphate | 20% $P_2O_5$ | 8 |
| Potassium Chloride | 60% $K_2O$ | 114 |
| Potassium Sulfate | 50% $K_2O$ | 46 |
| Dolomite | 30% CaO | 1 |
| | 20% MgO | |
| Gypsom | 33% CaO | 8 |
| Epsom Salts | 16% MgO | 44 |

plant's environment. Soluble fertilizer materials may be used at any time of the year with minimal risk of damage to turf if the factors that contribute to a burn are understood. The salt index of a fertilizer material is extremely important, especially when the fertilizer is highly soluble. The rates of application must be lower when a fertilizer with a high salt index is used, basically because of the salt effect.

Fertilizers with a low salt index should be used when soil test results indicate the presence of excessive levels of soluble salts in the soil. This can be a real problem in many areas. All plants react to salt problems just as the grass plant does.

# SUMMARY

1. Use a fertilizer that has a nutrient ratio of 3-1-2 or 4-1-2.

2. Do not apply a quickly available fertilizer at rates any higher than 1 pound of actual nitrogen per 1,000 square feet.

3. Do not fertilize a lawn during periods of dormancy or during environmental stress.

4. Quickly available fertilizers should be applied every four to six weeks while slowly available fertilizers should be applied every six to eight weeks during periods when the lawn is actively growing.

5. Divide the first number of the analysis into 100. Apply that many pounds for each 1,000 square feet of your lawn. (i.e. If you select a 19-5-9, 100 divided by 19 equals 5. So apply 5 pounds for each 1,000 square feet of lawn.)

# VIII
## WEED
## CONTROL

It is very possible that the most serious and perhaps the most frustrating pest problem associated with a lawn is that of weeds. No lawn is immune to them. Weeds are the opportunists of the plant world. A weed is ready to take advantage of any failure in the lawn's maintenance or at least it seems to be that way. In considering weed controls, there are a couple of facts you should know. First, weed seed is all over the place, in virtually every soil; secondly, weed seed can live in the soil for years and years just waiting for a chance to germinate.

In developing a weed control program there is absolutely no question that the front line in the " Weed War" is the adherence to a good lawn maintenance program that produces a thick, dense turf. Weeds rarely invade a high-quality lawn. All the money in the world can be spent on weed-controlling chemicals, but if the lawn is not maintained properly, chances are the weeds will return.

Once a weed is in place it must be removed either mechanically by digging or chemically. If the choice is by digging, all the underground parts of the weed that are capable of growing a new plant, such as the rhizome, must be removed. Rhizomes may extend undetected from above the soil to several inches or even a foot beyond

**Table 8-1**
**TYPES OF WEEDS**

| Grassy Weeds | | Broadleaf Weeds | |
| --- | --- | --- | --- |
| **Annuals** | **Perennials** | **Annuals** | **Perennials** |
| crabgrass | dallisgrass | henbit | dandelion |
| goosegrass | Johnsongrass | spurge | clover |
| annual bluegrass | nutgrass | aster | mouse-ear chickweed |
| sand bur | | | |

the base of the weed. If not completely removed, the weed will re-establish itself in a short period of time. Generally, perennial weeds have underground parts like rhizomes, while annual weeds do not.

When considering chemical control, it should be remembered that a chemical that is toxic to plants is being used to remove an undesirable plant (the weed) from a population of desirable plants (the lawn). Sometimes this is difficult. An example of this process is the fact that it takes more MSMA to kill common bermuda than it does to kill crabgrass, so if the proper rates of MSMA are used, the crabgrass will die and the worst that happens to the bermuda is that it gets a little yellow for a while.

Sometimes, weeds are very hard to control even though the right chemical is applied properly. Basically, the chemical which can kill the weed must enter the plant either through tiny openings in the leaves or through the root system. If it is a hot and dry day, these leaf openings may be closed and if soil moisture levels are low, the root system might not take up the chemical. The rule of thumb is that the weed must be actively growing for it to be controlled. A cooler day a few days after a good rain might be a prime time for weed control. A lot of weed control failures can be traced to unfavorable weather conditions. Also, the younger a weed is, the easier it is to control. Old weeds can be very tough.

There must be hundreds and hundreds of plants that one time or another could be called a weed. Weeds are both annual and perennial plants. They are either grass-like in their appearance or they are called a broad-leaf. (See Table 8-1.)

**Oxalis (top), Johnsongrass (bottom left) and white clover (bottom right) are common weeds in Texas lawns.**

Nutgrass (top left and continuing clockwise), thistle, spurge and goose grass can be controlled with the proper applications of an approved herbicide.

# CHEMICALS

Commonly available weed-control chemicals may be divided into two large groups—those that kill the weed seed as it germinates (called pre-emergent herbicides) and those that control the weed after it germinates (post-emergent herbicides).

# PRE-EMERGENT WEED CONTROL

With pre-emergent weed controls, a chemical is applied evenly over the lawn and forms a barrier at the soil surface. No germinating seed, be it weed or even grass seed, can penetrate this barrier without being killed. If not disturbed, the barrier can remain in place from a few months up to over a year. The type of soil and the amount of water used on the lawn has a lot to do with the life of the barrier.

The biggest problem with the use of pre-emergent herbicides is that of timing. The chemical must be in place before the weed seed begins to grow and the beginning of weed growth usually is tied to the weather patterns. There are a whole host of annuals, like henbit and annual bluegrass, that germinate in the fall as soon as the weather cools off. There could be as much as a month or so difference in the arrival of the first significant cold front. This means that in most years for a pre-emergent to be effective in North Texas, it should be applied around September 15 and a month or so later in the southern part of the state.

The same situation is present in the spring. Many annuals, like knotweed and crabgrass, germinate in early spring, again depending on temperatures. In northern Texas the pre-emergent herbicide should be applied by March 1 and, of course, even earlier further south. But there are years when these dates may be too late. The success of a good pre-emergent program, aside from considerations like using the proper rate and obtaining an even distribution, depends on changes in the weather. Early or late falls, and early or late springs make pre-emergent programs difficult. All that can be done is to follow the averages and accept the fact that once in a while the program may fail.

Chemicals that are used as pre-emergent herbicides are shown in Table 8-2.

# POST EMERGENT WEED CONTROL

Post-emergent chemicals are used to control weeds after they come up. Weeds, for control purposes, are divided into two groups—those that are grassy in appearance and the broadleaf types.(See Table 8-1.)

When selecting a post-emergent chemical, care must be given to make sure the chemical will control the weed without harming the lawn or any ornamental plants in or near the lawn. This is very important: the chemical formulator means what it says on the label.

**Table 8-2**
**CHEMICAL AND BRAND NAMES OF HERBICIDES**

| Chemical Name | Brand Name |
| --- | --- |
| Benefin | Balan |
| Bensulide | Betasan |
| DCPA | Dacthal |
| Simazine | Princep (fall only) |

# GRASSY WEED CONTROL

These are the hardest of the weeds to control because there just aren't many chemicals available that can selectively remove the grassy weed from among the desirable turfgrass plants. The only chemicals available to homeowners that do a fairly good job of killing grassy weeds in common bermudagrass lawns are MSMA (monosodium methanearsonate) or DSMA (disodium methanearsonate). Even these chemicals will need to be applied two or three times at the label rates to get a kill, and they may severely damage any turfgrasses other than common bermuda and buffalograss.

Grassy weeds may be removed from other lawns using a non-selective herbicide, such as a Roundup, Kleen-up or Doomsday. Each of these is formulated from a chemical called glyphosate and it may kill the lawn grass the spray gets on as well as the weed. Turfgrasses that spread, such as St. Augustine, should quickly fill in any dead spots created by the herbicide.

# BROADLEAF WEED CONTROL

There are several chemicals that can do a good job of controlling broadleaf weeds in any lawn. The chemicals most used in the various formulations available are 2,4-D, MCPP (mecoprop) and dicamba. Listed on each of the containers is a list of the broadleaf weeds, the formulation controls and which of the turfgrasses won't be harmed. Also, look for any warning concerning the use of the chemical around ornamental plants.

Henbit (top) and dallisgrass (bottom) can spread rapidly if not controlled.

# COMBINATION PRODUCTS

There are a number of combination fertilizer/herbicide products offered on the market. Most are a combination of fertilizer and a pre-emergent herbicide. These generally are good products that, if applied properly, do the job they say they will do. The only real problem with them is that of timing. As an example, if a pre-emergent herbicide must

Some weeds can be controlled with spot spraying (top photo). The dandelion (bottom) has been sprayed with a broadleaf herbicide.

**Black medic (top) and purslane (bottom) are two weeds that can be a serious problem in your lawn.**

be applied on or before March 1 to be effective on a bermudagrass lawn, it could well be too early to fertilize that lawn. Generally, bermuda won't be actively growing until April and the fertilizer could be gone by then. Usually, the right time to apply a herbicide is not the right time to fertilize.

# LIQUID VS. DRY

Some herbicides are offered in both liquid and dry forms. Since pre-emergent herbicides must be watered into the soil, it makes little difference which form is used. Just read and follow the label instructions.

Liquid post-emergent herbicides generally are considered to be superior to any dry or granular forms of the same chemical. Since most of these herbicides must enter the plant through the leaves, coating the leaf with a liquid increases the chances of killing the weed.

# IX

## INSECT
## CONTROL

Most lawns are full of insects of every description almost all the time. The good news is that very few insects feed on the turfgrass plant. Those that do, however, can cause serious injury in a short period of time. You should remember that most of the insects listed below will be present in any given lawn from time to time without being discovered or causing any apparent damage. It is only when their populations reach extremely high levels that you need to begin control measures.

### BELOW-GROUND INSECTS

**GRUBS:** These are the immature forms of several species of beetles. There are dozens of species of grubs and one kind or another can be found in any soil almost any time of the year, but very few of them feed on turfgrass roots. Those that do usually are not a problem until mid to late summer.

Since most turfgrass plants have a fairly extensive root system, it takes a very high grub population to cause any significant damage. Fewer than four or five grubs per square foot usually do not present a problem and treatment is not recommended. This number of grubs

**Grubworms (top) can do significant damage to your lawn (bottom) only if they are abundant in large numbers.**

certainly is not absolute. If a lawn is healthy and the root system is actively growing, the lawn possibly could support a much higher grub population without any bad effects.

Grubs feed on roots so the visual damage looks like grass that needs to be watered, but these grub-infested areas will not respond easily to water because most of the root system is gone. When this type of damage is observed, a shovel and a little digging should reveal the grubs. Treatment with a recommended insecticide is in order.

To be effective, the insecticide must reach the grub. If the soil is poorly drained, or if there is any kind of thatch layer present, it may not be easy to get the insecticide down to the grubs. A wetting agent may help the downward movement of the chemical.

Mole crickets (top) and ground pearls both attack the grass plant's root system.

Another point to remember is that some of the grubs may be in a resting stage in their life cycle and cannot be controlled which, along with failure to get the insecticide through any thatch layer or a heavy soil, are the prime reasons for failure to control grubs.

**MOLE CRICKETS:** These rather large insects burrow through the soil and feed on turfgrass roots. They can be up to 1½ inches in length and seem to have a preference for sandier soils, which make burrowing easier. Their tunnels or burrows look like very small mole tunnels and are visual evidence of their presence. Like grubs, a few mole crickets won't do much damage, but when several tunnels are seen in a small area it's time to treat.

**GROUND PEARLS:** These are small scale insects, measuring up to ⅛ inch across, that attach and feed on the grass plant's root

Sod webworms (top) and cutworms both feed at the base of turfgrass plants.

system. They protect themselves by forming a pearl-like shell around their bodies, making it nearly impossible to control them with an insecticide. The visual evidence of their presence, like that of other root-feeding insects, is brown spots that do not respond to water. If dug up, ground pearls will be found still attached to the roots.

# ABOVEGROUND INSECTS

**SOD-WEBWORMS:** These insects live in small tunnels of silk and are located in a thatch layer or in the soil. At night, they feed on the base of the grass plant. Intense feeding can damage a lawn seriously.

**Armyworms (top) and chinch bugs (bottom) feed on the blades of grass leaves.**

Bermudagrass mites are too small to see but you can see their damage as in the top photo. The mites will feed on the bottom parts of the grass plant, eventually killing large areas if not controlled. Scale insects such as the mealybug (bottom) usually are not a problem but can be difficult to control.

Leaves cut off at the base of the plant are a sign that sod webworms may be present.

**CUTWORMS:** Cutworms, like sod webworms, also feed at the base of the turfgrass plant but they do not build tunnels. They appear in early spring, feed at night and are found in the soil during the day. Leaves and stems are cut off but may not be eaten.

**ARMYWORMS:** These are caterpillars, measuring 1½ inches long, that have distinctive stripes along the sides of their body. They feed on grass leaf blades.

**CHINCH BUGS:** These usually are found during hot, dry weather and feed primarily on St. Augustine. There are, however, varieties of St. Augustine that have some resistance to chinch bugs. (See Chapter 1.) The nymphs and adults feed on the turfgrass plant by

---

**Table 9-1**
**CHEMICAL CONTROLS FOR INSECTS**

| Insects | Chemical |
|---|---|
| Below-ground Insects | Diazinon |
| | Dursban |
| | Oftanol |
| Use wetting agents to aid penetration. | Use label rates and water in well. |
| Aboveground Insects | |
| Armyworms | Carbaryl |
| | Diazinon |
| | Malathion |
| | *Bacillus Thuringiensis* |
| Cutworms | Carbaryl (baits) |
| | Dursban |
| | Diazinon |
| Sod Webworms | Diazinon |
| and Chinch Bugs | Dursban |
| | Carbaryl |
| Mites | Diazinon* |
| | Kelthane* |

*Use spray formulation and wet grass thoroughly using 3 to 5 gallons of water per 1,000 square feet. A wetting agent may improve control.

---

sucking plant juices. The first symptom is chlorosis and the affected plant rapidly turns brown.

One of the easiest ways to test for chinch bugs is to insert a coffee can that has been opened at both ends about an inch or so into the soil and then fill it with water. Any chinch bugs present will float to the surface. The adults are black and white and about ¼ inch long while the smaller nymphs are reddish in color.

**BERMUDAGRASS MITES:** These are very small ''insects'' that feed on the bottom parts of the plant. Their feeding results in the development of abnormal growth patterns at the node of the bermudagrass stolon. The growth, which still may be green at first, takes on a tufted appearance. As feeding increases, the grass will die and it's not uncommon for mites to kill areas several feet wide if not controlled.

**SCALE INSECTS:** These small insects attach themselves to the leaf stem and form a protective covering, making control nearly impossible. Their occurrence is fairly rare and usually not a problem.

# X

# DISEASE
# CONTROL

It takes two things to have a turf disease problem—the right environmental conditions and a turfgrass that is susceptible to that particular disease. With one exception, all turfgrass diseases are caused by fungi and each fungi has a fairly set range of temperatures and humidities in which it can operate. The one exception is the viral disease of St. Augustine called St. Augustine Decline (SAD).

Most fungi can be controlled chemically, but many times fungi-caused diseases are controlled by a change in the weather rather than by chemicals. Since very high humidities are needed for fungi growth, a drop in the humidity may end disease activity. In reverse, if the humidity stays high, the disease pressure can be so great that no chemical can stop the disease activity. In areas with normally low summer humidity about the only way for a lawn to get a disease is to water it too much. (There are, of course, exceptions to this rule of thumb.)

The chemicals used to prevent or control disease are called fungicides. There are two basic types of fungicides available. Some are called *contact* fungicides because they coat the leaves of the turfgrass

**Helminthosporium, shown at top in a Tall Fescue lawn, also attacks bermudagrass and ryegrass. Brown Patch (bottom) is a disease of St. Augustine lawns.**

plant with a chemical that kills a fungi when it comes in contact. During periods of high disease activity, a contact-type fungicide may need to be re-applied every week or so because leaves that have been coated with the fungicide grow and are mowed off and the new leaves have no fungicide protection. The other type of fungicide is *systemic*. That is the chemicals enter the plant and kill the fungus as it tries to invade the plant. These fungicides may be effective for up to three or four weeks.

A fungus is a plant that has no chlorophyll and cannot produce its own food like green plants do. In order to feed, it must enter a green plant. Fungi live in or near the soil as spores, waiting for the right weather and the right plant to come along.

# COMMON DISEASES

**HELMINTHOSPORIUM:** This is a fairly common leaf spot disease, usually found on bermudagrass, tall fescue and ryegrass. The small spots on the leaf blade are brown in the middle with a dark ring. One or two of these infections on a plant's leaf will not seriously hurt it, but as more develop, the leaf's ability to produce food is reduced and the plant becomes weaker. A lawn with a serious infection of "helminth" will slowly thin out. This disease also has been called "fading out" or "thinning out."

**BROWN PATCH:** This is one of the fairly common diseases of St. Augustine, although it can be a problem on bermudagrass, too. The leaves of the grass plants are killed in a circular area. Spots may be up to several feet in diameter. The dead giveaway for this disease is that the affected leaves can be easily pulled off the runners. Brown patch usually is not fatal as far as the plant is concerned. It is mostly present in spring and fall during periods of frequent rain and, of course, high humidity. As the weather gets warmer and drier, leaves are again produced by the runners and the lawn recovers. One fairly serious side-effect of brown patch is that while the leaves of the plant are non-functional during an infection, the rest of the plant is not receiving any food material. The manufacturing and storage of food material is fairly critical during the fall since the plant is getting ready for winter dormancy. It is not uncommon for areas that have had brown patch during the previous fall to be the victims of winter kill.

**GRAY LEAF SPOT:** This is another disease that can infect St. Augustine. It's much like helminthosporium in that the infected spot on the leaf is surrounded by a dark margin. Here again, a few spots won't necessarily do any harm, but a lot will.

**RUST:** This is a disease that can be found on most turfgrasses, although zoysia may be the most severely affected. The rust develops orange or brown pustules on the leaves. If you get enough of these on a leaf, the plant's ability to manufacture food is reduced and the turf thins out.

**SPRING DEAD SPOT:** These are simply circular spots of bermudagrass that do not green up in the spring. The grass in these spots died sometime during the winter. The organisms which cause this problem have never been identified. The turfgrass will be slow to spread back into these areas. It may take all of the next summer for the dead spots to fill in completely. Usually, seeds will not germinate in these areas for a year or so. Lawns that get spring dead spots usually have been on very high fertility programs, especially those programs that are high in nitrogen.

**NIGROSPORA:** This is a disease primarily of St. Augustine. It affects the stolon, or runner. A small lesion develops that looks much like the leaf spot diseases. The spot grows larger and larger until it completely encircles the runner. This results in the death of all the new plants between the lesion and the end of the runner. It can be a very serious disease that certainly can be promoted by over-watering.

**ST. AUGUSTINE DECLINE:** This is a serious viral disease of St. Augustine. There is no cure. The lawn will more than likely go through a long, steady decline as more and more plants are infected. Leaves take on a spotty or mottled appearance. A good management program will prolong the life of the affected lawn, but the end is inevitable. The only realistic way to deal with St. Augustine Decline is to begin to introduce SAD-resistant varieties into the lawn. Those that have demonstrated resistance are Floratam, Seville and Raleigh.

**FAIRY RING:** These appear as circles, or arcs, of dark green grass in any lawn. The mushrooms, or fruiting bodies, of the soilborne fungi that cause fairy ring may or may not appear. The dark ring is caused by the breakdown of organic material deep into the soil by the fungi. There is no chemical control or cure for this disease. A good fertility program usually will "mask" the rings and they shouldn't be as evident.

**Common turfgrass diseases to watch for are (clockwise from top left) gray leaf spot, rust, spring dead spot and nigrospora.**

**Other common turfgrass diseases are (clockwise from top left) St. Augustine decline, fairy ring, pythium blight and slime mold.**

**Table 10-1**
**DISEASE CONTROLS**

| Disease | Fungicide |
|---|---|
| 1. Helminthosporium | Tersan LSR |
|  | Fore |
|  | Daconil 2787 |
|  | Chipco 26019 (ROVRAL |
| 2. Brown Patch | Teraclor (PCNB) |
|  | Daconil 2787 |
|  | *Fungo 50 |
|  | *Tersan 1991 |
|  | Chipco 26019 (ROVRAL) |
| 3. Gray Leaf Spot | Fore |
|  | Daconil 2787 |
|  | Chipco 26019 (ROVRAL) |
| 4. Rust | *Bayleton |
|  | Zineb |
|  | Wettable Sulfer |
| 5. Nigrospora | Daconil 2787 |
| 6. Pythium | Koban |
|  | Tersan SP |
|  | Truban |

*Systemic

**PYTHIUM:** Pythium can be a serious disease of both perennial ryegrass and bermudagrass. It can develop under warm and very wet conditions, especially in low areas of the lawn. The grass takes on a wilted, greasy look at first. Later some spots may have a cottony appearance and, for this reason, the disease may be called cottony blight. The spots may be small circles or they may be streaked. Over-watering may be one of the reasons this disease develops.

**SLIME MOLDS:** These molds can cover the aboveground parts of the plant with a dusty dark gray mass. While slime molds are not too common, it is not uncommon to find them growing on bermudagrass seed heads. There is no chemical control and they usually disappear when the weather becomes drier. They tend to develop during wetter weather.

# CHEMICAL CONTROLS

Most fungicide labels will have two application rates. One is a preventative rate that when applied should help keep the disease from developing. This rate may be used during periods of the year when the environmental conditions are favorable for disease development. For example, during spring or fall a fungicide could be applied to St. Augustine lawns to help prevent brown patch.

The other rate is much higher and is a curative rate. This is applied after the disease is present and has been diagnosed. (See Table 10-1 for recommended controls of turfgrass disease.)

# XI
# AERIFICATION

Every lawn has some amount of traffic on it from time to time. The traffic may only amount to an occasional mowing or it may be some daily athletic event, such as touch football. Lawns that are trafficiked are subject to soil compaction. The more traffic, the more compaction.

Compaction is a physical process which slowly reduces the amount of oxygen contained in a soil. (See Figure 11-1.) The roots of the turfgrass plant need oxygen and, as a product of their growth process, give off carbon dioxide. Oxygen from the atmosphere moves into the soil through very small pores to the roots of the plant. Carbon dioxide escapes up through the soil into the atmosphere. As the soil is trafficked, the soil particles in the top inch or two are compacted so that less and less oxygen can enter the soil and less and less carbon dioxide can escape. The net result is a thinner and thinner turf until, ultimately, the soil can no longer support any turf growth at all. An amazing number of weeds can grow in these compacted soils where the grasses can't grow.

Since compaction is the result of a physical process, it takes

**Thinning out is a common sign that a lawn needs aerification.**

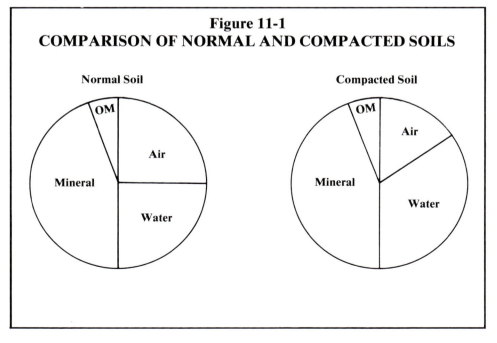

**Figure 11-1**
**COMPARISON OF NORMAL AND COMPACTED SOILS**

Normal Soil

OM
Air
Mineral
Water

Compacted Soil

OM
Air
Mineral
Water

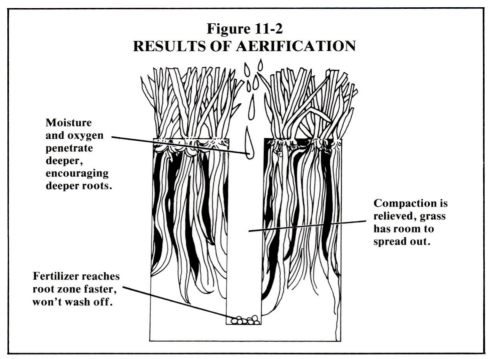

**Figure 11-2**
**RESULTS OF AERIFICATION**

Moisture and oxygen penetrate deeper, encouraging deeper roots.

Compaction is relieved, grass has room to spread out.

Fertilizer reaches root zone faster, won't wash off.

another physical process to reduce its effects. There are machines, usually simply called "aerifiers," that have a number of hollow or open metal tubes called "tines" that can be used to relieve compaction. The tines are about ½ inch in diameter and when the machine is operated, penetrate the soil to a depth of 2 or 3 inches. As the tine is pulled up out of the soil, a soil core is removed. These are deposited on the surface of the lawn and after a few waterings they will dissipate. The holes left in the lawn become an avenue for oxygen to once again penetrate deeply into the soil and for carbon dioxide to escape. Root growth around the hole is greatly increased and the vigor of plants around the hole is greatly enhanced. Then, the greater the number of holes poked into the lawn, the greater the increase in that lawn's vigor. (See Figure 11-2.)

The frequency at which a lawn may need to be aerified is solely dependent on the amount of traffic it receives and to some extent the texture of the soil under the lawn. A lawn that has no more traffic than foot traffic associated with the normal maintenance program and

**An aerifier (top) is used to remove the soil core, allowing aerification to occur.**

perhaps an occasional football game should never need any
aerification. When traffic becomes heavy enough to thin the lawn out
it is time to aerify. Heavily trafficked areas may need to be aerified
at least two or three times a year.

      The best time to aerify is when the lawn is actively growing. The
roots will fill the holes rapidly and the lawn will recover faster. If the
lawn is aerified during its dormant period, the open holes may allow the
excessive loss of soil moisture. Any lawn may be aerified, regardless of
the turfgrass variety.

# XII
## THATCH
## CONTROL

Most turfgrasses are perennial plants that live in a continuous state of renewal. New plants are produced and old plants die. Ideally, under proper management, the lawn achieves a balance between the rate at which organic matter is produced and the rate at which it is decomposed. This organic matter does have value. It contains various plant nutrients which, after decomposition by micro-organisms, may be returned to the soil for possible future use by new turfgrass plants.

## WHAT IS THATCH?

When organic material is produced faster than it can be decomposed, the lawn develops thatch. Thatch primarily consists of partially decomposed stem and root tissue and some living stem and root tissues that develop in the organic layer between the base of the turfgrass plant and soil. (See Figure 12-1.) Stem, crown and root tissues are high in cell material that's very hard to decompose. The leaves cut off in the mowing process are rapidly decomposed by bacteria and fungi and do not contribute to thatch.

A certain amount of thatch is desirable, because it forms a cushion in the lawn to increase wear tolerance. Since most lawns are

**A special vertical mower can be used to remove thatch build-up, but usually isn't necessary if a lawn is maintained properly.**

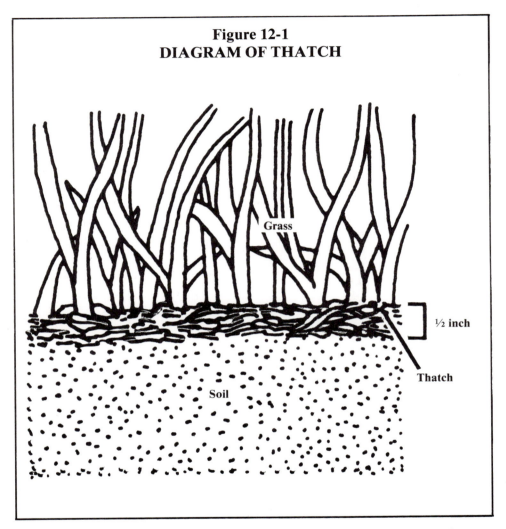

**Figure 12-1**
**DIAGRAM OF THATCH**

Grass

½ inch

Thatch

Soil

subjected to traffic, thatch helps the lawn withstand the wear and tear associated with moderate levels of traffic. Thatch also insulates the soil from high temperatures and reduces water evaporation losses from the surface of the soil. To be desirable, the thatch layer should not exceed about ¼ inch. When thatch accumulates more than ¼ inch, problems usually develop. A heavy thatch layer may seriously reduce water movement into the soil. It also may reduce soil aeration which is necessary for good root growth. Increased disease and insect problems are at times associated with a heavy thatch layer. Also, a thatch layer in excess of ¼ inch can create a barrier for the movement of fertilizer and insecticides (such as those used for grub control) into the soil.

# WHY DOES THATCH ACCUMULATE?

It's a fact that some lawns tend to develop thatch fairly easily and some do not. One reason is that the turfgrasses vary in their tendency to thatch.

There are several basic causes for thatch build-up in a lawn. Improper use of water can encourage a problem and lawns that are excessively watered, especially those watered daily, tend to develop heavy thatch. Heavy use of pesticides on a lawn also may promote thatch accumulation by destroying many of the organisms that decompose thatch.

Perhaps the major cause of thatch build-up is the use of high rates of soluble nitrogen fertilizers. Nitrogen is a plant nutrient that stimulates vegetative growth of turfgrass. As stated previously, in an ideal lawn management system the growth rate of the lawn should equal the rate at which the turfgrass residues are decomposed. Because of the strong influence of soluble nitrogen on growth, excessive application rates add plant residues to the system faster than they can be decomposed. As a result, thatch accumulates in the lawn.

Improper mowing also can lead to a thatch problem. The lawn should be mowed when the height of the grass is about one and a half times greater than the height setting of the mower. That is, if the mower is set for 2 inches, the lawn should be cut when it is no higher than 3 inches. This practice fits the basic "rule of thumb" for mowing that states that "no more than one-third of the leaf surface area should be removed at one time." If a lawn is mowed at the right frequency, the clippings may be left to fall back into the turf and they will decompose rapidly. The frequency at which a lawn should be mowed is determined by the growth rate. The use of a mulching mower may help prevent a problem. While a mulching mower will not cut back on how often you need to mow, it may well speed up the rate at which leaf tissue is decomposed by chopping up the leaves into smaller particles.

Vertical mowers will cut into the soil, leaving slight ridges visible in the lawn.

# HOW TO CHECK FOR THATCH

A lawn that has too much thatch is spongy. Mowers tend to scalp lawns that have excessive thatch. To estimate the depth of thatch, use a knife, spade or soil probe to remove a small section of turf. Make sure the cut extends deep enough to go through the thatch layer to the true surface of the soil. Measure the amount of thatch. If it is thicker than ¼ inch, the lawn should be de-thatched.

# HOW TO REMOVE THATCH

The best time to remove thatch is in spring before the lawn turns green. Machines specifically designed for the removal of thatch are called vertical mowers (because the blades rotate vertically), power rakes or dethatching mowers. In using this type of equipment, make sure the blades, or knives, penetrate through the thatch to the surface of the soil. On St. Augustine lawns, the knives should be spaced 2 or 3 inches apart; on bermudagrass lawns they may be 1 to 1½ inches apart.

The lawn should be vertically mowed in one or two directions, each time removing the material brought up by the mower.

Another means of thatch control is to lower the height of the lawn mower's blade for the first cutting in the spring. Mow the lawn in several directions, removing the dead material after each mowing. Scalping the lawn in this manner is not as effective as using a vertical mower. Consider using any thatch picked up from the lawn in a compost pile rather than adding it to already over-crowded landfills.

# HOW TO PREVENT THATCH

The most desirable method of thatch control is to prevent its accumulation. The following suggestions will be of help:

1. Avoid applying soluble nitrogen fertilizers at rates higher than 1 pound of nitrogen per 1,000 square feet per application.

2. Water thoroughly (wet the soil to a depth of 4 to 6 inches), and water only when the lawn needs it.

3. Avoid the use of pesticides as much as possible. Treat only when a pest is present and has or may become a problem.

4. Adjust the frequency of mowing so that no more than a third of the leaf surface is removed at any one mowing.

5. Remove tree leaves when they accumulate on the surface.

# XIII
## WINTER
## LAWNS

**M**any, many lawns in Texas are established from warm-season turfgrasses like bermuda, centipede or buffalograss seed each year. This is all well and good but an unfortunate fact is that there is a rather limited part of the year when the success rate of using seed for the establishment of these turfgrasses is high.

Another problem to consider is that many new homes are completed and occupied during periods when seeding these warm-season turfgrasses is not realistic. (See Chapter 4.) It's possible that it may be as much as six months before a lawn can be seeded for homes that were completed and occupied in late summer. That's a long time to fight the mud and dust that can be tracked into the home and a long time for the kids and pets to play on bare soil. Added to all this is the fact that these bare lawns are subjected to an extended period of erosion. It's very possible that any topsoil left by the final grading operation could be completely lost and end up either in the street or down the storm sewer before a lawn can be started.

However, you can seed these newly completed lawns with a plant that will provide temporary erosion control and help keep

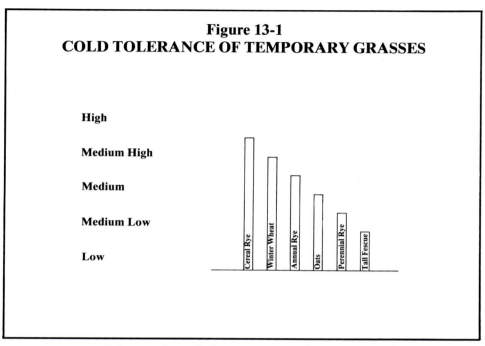

**Figure 13-1**
**COLD TOLERANCE OF TEMPORARY GRASSES**

High

Medium High

Medium

Medium Low

Low

Cereal Rye — Winter Wheat — Annual Rye — Oats — Perennial Rye — Tall Fescue

everyone out of the mud until the warm weather returns. Some of the plants available for this purpose are the northern, or cool-season, turfgrasses and a few plants that are ''grass-like'' in their nature. The selection of one of these varieties should be based on the current weather temperature. As the temperature gets colder, a plant lower on the list should be used.

After the ideal period of the year to seed a permanent turfgrass has passed, tall fescue or perennial ryegrass can be used. As time passes and it gets colder, it would be well to use plants lower on the list. (See Figure 13-1.) Cereal rye will germinate the best in the coolest part of the year. If it won't come up, nothing will come up. This seed can be found, but it might be necessary to check with a farm supply store for some varieties.

Minimum seedbed preparation is necessary for these plants and they should be seeded at a rate of about 2 pounds per 1,000 square feet. As soon as they get about 3 inches high they should be cut at 2 inches. Because these are temporary lawns, fertilizer may not be necessary.

Most of these varieties will die out when warm temperatures

**Depending on how cold it is when you plant, temporary winter lawns can be established from grasses such as cereal rye. Such lawns usually are planted by new homeowners who move in too late in the year to establish a permanent lawn.**

return in late spring, but if they haven't died by the time to seed one of the permanent turfgrasses, they can be killed out with chemicals such as Roundup or Kleen-up. The stubble left behind by the dead temporary lawn can now act as a mulch for the new seeding. You can just seed into the dead stubble. The dead plants will decompose as the permanent turfgrass begins to grow.

# WINTER COLOR

If you don't care to look at that brown lawn all winter, you really don't have to. The lawn can be green all winter long if you overseed it with either a perennial ryegrass or with rough bluegrass *(Poa trivialis)*. The best period to overseed is about one month before the lawn normally turns brown.

The suggested overseeding rates for perennial ryegrass is about 5 pounds per 1,000 square feet and for rough bluegrass, no more than 2 pounds per 1,000 square feet. The best way to prepare a lawn for overseeding is to use a vertical mower. A series of vertical knives will open up avenues for the seed to reach the soil. After applying the seed, begin frequent light waterings to keep the seed moist until it germinates. As the new grass plants emerge, gradually reduce the watering frequency until it's back to normal.

Set your mower for 2 inches and begin to mow when your new grass reaches about 3 inches in height. Fertilize with a 3-1-2 ratio material, such as 12-4-8 or 15-5-10, at a rate of about 7 pounds per 1,000 square feet prior to overseeding and again about six weeks later if needed. Cool weather will slow down the growth rate of the lawn so it will have a relatively low fertilizer requirement the rest of the winter season and it shouldn't need a lot of mowing.

Your overseeding should slowly die out next spring with the return of warm weather and the permanent summer lawn grass will take over. The worst that can happen is that the overseed grass might remain healthy after the permanent grasses begin to green up and may need to be removed chemically.

# XIV
## COMMON PROBLEM QUESTIONS

**1. How often should I water?**

The easy answer is not to water any more than is absolutely necessary. Wait until the soil is dry 2 or 3 inches deep and then water until the soil is wetted 4 to 6 inches deep. All lawns are different and the proper watering program should be based on experience. Put the longest possible interval between waterings. Over-watering can lead to disease, thatch, weed invasion and poor growth. (See Chapter 6 for more information.)

**2. Which fertilizer is best?**

There are a number of good fertilizers available and many will do a fine job. Unless a soil test or qualified local expert indicates otherwise, research has shown a 3-1-2 ratio fertilizer, such as 15-5-10 or 12-4-8, will do a good job on any turfgrass any time of the year. (See Chapter 7 for more information.)

### 3. Do I need a soil test?

It certainly won't hurt to get a soil test. Most university or extension service recommendations are based on years of hundreds of soil tests. If you feel your lawn is different than most others, then a soil test might help. See your local county extension agent for help. (See Chapter 3 for more information.)

### 4. What should I plant in the shade?

The choice is basically St. Augustine, zoysia or tall fescue. If none of these will grow, then a ground cover should be considered. (See Chapter 1 for more information.)

### 5. My lawn has brown spots—what's wrong?

There could be any one of several things wrong. It could be a disease, but only if the lawn has been fairly wet for a long period of time. Grubs or other insects could cause them, but you should be able to find the insects if they are present. The spots could be the result of the lawn being too dry. If you have brown spots, read about each possibility and you might be able to pin down the specific cause. (See Chapters 6, 9 and 10 for more information.)

### 6. My bermuda gets stemmy late in the summer. Should I raise the mower?

This is a very common occurrence in bermuda lawns. If the lawn is cut the right mowing height and often enough, it shouldn't happen. Either lower the mower and cut more often or you will need to raise the mower throughout the late summer to keep from scalping. (See Chapter 5 for more information.)

### 7. When can I seed Common bermuda?

You can seed Common bermudagrass or even U3 bermuda when the soil temperature a few inches below the surface reaches about

One possible cause of spots forming on your lawn is frost damage (top photo). Scalping a bermudagrass lawn can be avoided by mowing it often enough and by setting your mower at the appropriate height.

65 degrees. That is usually late April in North Texas, but it may be a month earlier further south. The end of the seeding period is harder to determine. To be as sure as possible, the only fair statement is that in northern Texas the odds of successfully establishing a seeded lawn well enough to get through the first winter begin to go downhill the last part of August and by September 15 the season is over. Seeding can last longer, of course, further south.

### 8. What is the recommended seeding rate for buffalograss?

Buffalograss seed as compared to other grass seed is expensive and larger in size. This means there is not that many seeds per pound. Bermudagrass has something like 1,500,000 seeds per pound while buffalograss has around 50,000. If the rate for bermudagrass is 1 pound per 1,000 square feet (and that's reasonable), it would take 30 pounds of buffalograss to have the same number of plants. Since bermuda sells for about $3 a pound and buffalograss for about $10 a pound, the best answer to this question is how much you can afford.

### 9. How can I get dallisgrass out of St. Augustine?

The only way is to spot spray it or physically remove it. Use a glyphosate and try not to get any more on the St. Augustine than is absolutely necessary. (See Chapter 8 for more information.)

### 10. When should I treat for grubs?

Grubs usually cause problems only in mid to late summer. Since most insecticides only last a short period, it's hard to expect one or even two applications to give season-long control. Be suspicious of brown or drying spots and look for grubs. When they are present—treat. (See Chapter 9 for more information.)

### 11. How can I get rid of sandburs?

These are annual plants that can be controlled with a pre-emergent herbicide applied in early spring. (See Chapter 8 for more information.)

### 12. How can I get rid of nutgrass?

This is about the hardest weed to eliminate. There is no chemical that will get it completely out of a lawn. Repeated applications may be necessary. Try MSMA or a glyphosate. (See Chapter 8 for more information.)

### 13. Are the ads in the Sunday paper for zoysia true?

Lots of ads we see are prepared for northern markets and while what they say may be true if comparing zoysia with bluegrass, it may not be as true if zoysia was compared to bermuda. Read them carefully. (See Chapter 1 for more information.)

### 14. Do I have to bag my grass clippings?

No, you sure don't. Read Chapter 5 and you'll see how to compost your clippings.

### 15. I only run the sprinkler for a little while, but the water runs off—what can I do?

There are two things you can try. Use an aerifier and/or use a wetting agent. A combination of both would be best. (See chapters 6 and 11 for more information.)

### 16. I have a large area I can't water—what should I plant?

The best choice probably is buffalograss, but Common bermudagrass will take to a fairly dry site too. (See Chapter 1 for more information.)

### 17. Should I sod, hydromulch or seed my lawn myself?

This is mostly an economic decision. Sod is quickest, but more expensive. Seed is cheapest, but slowest. Check all the prices before you pick one.

The same soil that already is in the lawn should be used to fill in low spots. You should not use sand over clay soil as in the photo above.

### 18. How can I stop those ugly bermuda seed heads?

There is no real sure way to prevent or stop seed heads. Increasing the level of nitrogen might help.

### 19. When is the best time to plant tall fescue?

The best time is early fall, around the first part of October. This will give it time to develop a good root system before winter. It will also

It's possible for grass to dry out over a sand pocket in the lawn.

have a good long growing period the following spring to mature before the plant has to face the summer heat. (See Chapters 1 and 4 for more information.)

### 20. My new bermudagrass has turned purple—what's wrong?

Reddish or purple seedling bermudagrass is a sign that it's being over-watered. Reduce watering and it should turn green again. (See Chapter 4 for more information.)

**21. When is the best time to level my yard and what should I use?**

The best time is early spring just before spring growth begins. The lawn can be scalped down at that time without any damage. That will make it easier to spread the soil. Use the same kind of soil as the existing lawn. If possible, mix the new soil with that underneath to prevent layering. Do not use sand unless the present soil is sand.

# XV
# BACKYARD
# PUTTING
# GREEN

There are very few golfers that at one time or another haven't wished they had their very own putting green in the backyard. How great it would be to brush up on the old putting stroke by simply walking out the back door. It's possible to have a putting green but, as they say, it takes a lot of work.

## SITE PREPARATION

A fairly circular area with no severe slopes should be selected. It also should not have any dramatic changes in elevation. Most "real" putting greens are around 5,000 or 6,000 square feet, so the size of the backyard green depends on the length of the putt you intend to practice. For a green to accommodate up to a 50-foot putt, it should be about 2,000 square feet.

All vegetation on the future green site should be completely killed out, using a product containing glyphosate, such as Roundup or Kleen-Up. The soil should be tilled to a depth of about 2 inches and then carefully smoothed out. The easiest way to get a putting surface would be to use sod. Sprigs can be used at a rate of about 10 bushels per 1,000 square feet.

# SELECTION OF TURFGRASS

There are really very few turfgrasses that can be used for a putting green. In the South, the choice is limited to one of the bermudagrasses. The names of those that could be used are: Tifdwarf, Tifgreen (328), Tifgreen II and PeeDee. While the selection of one of these may be limited just to which one is available locally, the best day-in-and-day-out choice is Tifgreen, also called "Tif 328."

# ESTABLISHMENT

If sod is used, just after it is laid it should be rolled to get it as smooth as possible and the rolling will help drive out any air that might be trapped under the soil. The next step is to soak the sod completely. Care should be taken to make sure the watering is long enough so that the soil under the sod is wet.

If the sprigs are used they should be applied evenly over the site and rolled. The rolling should help push some of the sprigs into the soil (which was loosened during site preparation). If possible, a thin layer (¼ to ½ inch) of soil should be evenly applied over the sprigs. The soil used should be the same soil as that which is present in the base of the green. A good soaking should complete the establishment operation.

# WATERING

The newly sodded green should next be watered when it begins to show water stress or wilt symptoms. Then it should be soaked with at least 1 inch of water. Sod will root quickly and a "normal" watering schedule can be followed in a week or so.

Sprigs will need to be watered more frequently than sod. The sprigs really must be kept moist. Not saturated, just moist. It probably will take sprigs about one month or so to fill in the green, then a "normal" watering schedule may be followed.

After the establishment period has passed, the green should get about ½ inch of water every three or four days. This schedule may not work at all, just because of variations in local climate and soil types, but it's a place to begin. The goal in watering is to put on as much water as possible at infrequent intervals. An in-ground irrigation system controlled by an automatic timer is highly desirable.

If you have the space, it is possible to install a backyard putting green but the green will require a high level of maintenance.

# MOWING

This operation may prove to be the hardest part of this whole putting green operation. There is just no getting around it, a reel-type mower must be used. It should be set at about ¼ inch cutting height and you must mow at least every other day. Every day would be better. Make sure the reel mower selected can cut at ¼-inch height and that it has at least seven blades on the reel. Any fewer blades and the green won't be very smooth. The density of the green will suffer if it is cut any higher or any less frequently than these recommendations indicate.

# FERTILIZATION

A fertility program need not be complicated just because it is a putting green. A good safe place to start is to to apply a 15-5-10 at a rate of about 3 pounds per 1,000 square feet every two weeks during the green's growing season. If this doesn't do the job and the green is not "green" enough or it's not growing well, then increase the rate by a pound or two per application. Really, the less fertilizer you can use and still maintain quality, the better off the green is in the long run.

# TOP-DRESSING

The nature of the kinds of turfgrass used for greens makes it necessary or desirable to apply a thin (up to ⅛ inch) top-dressing from time to time. The application of top-dressing will serve to smooth the green and also will aid in controlling any thatch development. The soil used for top-dressing should be basically the same soil present in the base of the green. Top-dressing one or two times during the growing season may be enough.

The hardest part will be the actual application of the top-dressing itself. Golf courses have specialized equipment for this operation, but the odds are that the backyard putting green owner won't have this type of equipment available. If the top-dressing is dry, a drop-type fertilizer spreader might do a fairly good job. A rotary-type spreader might be a second choice. After the top-dressing is applied, some type of a steel mat should be dragged repeatedly across the green at different angles. The mat will move top-dressing from the high spots to the low spots and thus help smooth the green.

# VERTICLE MOWING

Another operation that helps greens maintain quality is verticle mowing. This mower has a set of verticle rather than horizontal blades. It is used for thatch control and grain control. Grain of a golf green is simply a problem that develops when all the leaves tend to lay in the same direction. The verticle mower should be set so that the blades almost go down the soil surface. Like top-dressing, verticle mowing may be a once or twice-a-year operation during the growing season. Verticle mowers are available in many lawn equipment rental stores.

# PEST CONTROL

The odds are that this green will not have any more weed, insect or disease problems than the rest of the lawn. The turfgrasses used for greens generally are more susceptible to herbicide damage than other turfgrasses so it might be desirable to use a knife and just cut the weeds. A few hours spent cutting out weeds can prevent setting the green back.

If insects or disease problems should occur, note control recommendations in Chapters 9 and 10. Remember two of the greatest enemies the green can have are over-watering and over-fertilization.

# QUICK REFERENCE GUIDE
## COVERSION TABLE

1 acre = 43,560 square feet or 4,840 square yards.
1 square yard = 9 square feet.
1 cubic yard = 27 cubic feet or 202 gallons of water.
1 cubic foot = 144 cubic inches or 7.5 gallons of water.
1,000 square feet = 111 square yards.
1 cubic foot of water = 62 pounds.
1 cubic foot of sand = 90 pounds.

loam = 80 pounds.
clay = 75 pounds.

1 tablespoon = 3 teaspoons.
1 fluid ounce = 2 tablespoons.
1 cup = 16 tablespoons.
1 pint = 2 cups or 32 tablespoons.
1 quart = 2 pints or 4 cups or 64 tablespoons.
1 gallon = 4 quarts or 8 pints or 16 cups.
1 acre inch of water = 27,154 gallons.
1 inch of water on 1,000 sq. ft. = 624 gallons.

# QUICK REFERENCE GUIDES
## MOWING

| Lawn Type | Mower Setting | Height At Mowing* |
|---|---|---|
| Common Bermuda | 1½'' | 2¼'' |
| Hybrid Bermuda | 1'' | 1½'' |
| St. Augustine | 2'' | 3'' |
| Centipede | 1'' | |
| Tall Fescue | 2½ | 3½ |
| Zoysia | 2'' | 3'' |
| Buffalograss | 2'' | 3'' |
| Bluegrass | 2½ | 3½ |
| Temporary Lawn | 2'' | 3'' |

*You should mow when or before grass is the indicated height. For more information see Chapter 5.

# Quick Reference Guide
## Fertilizer Application Dates

| LAWN TYPE | 1/1 | 1/15 | 2/1 | 2/15 | 3/1 | 3/15 | 4/1 | 4/15 | 5/1 | 5/15 | 6/1 | 6/15 | 7/1 | 7/15 | 8/1 | 8/15 | 9/1 | 9/15 | 10/1 | 10/15 | 11/1 | 11/15 | 12/1 | 12/15 |
|---|---|---|---|---|---|---|---|---|---|---|---|---|---|---|---|---|---|---|---|---|---|---|---|---|
| * Common Bermuda | | | | | | | | X | | | X | | | X | | | X | | | | | | | |
| * Hybrid Bermuda | | | | | | | | X | | X | | X | | X | | X | | X | | | | | | |
| * St. Augustine | | | | | | | | X | | | X | | | | | | X | | | | | | | |
| Tall Fescue | | | | | X | | | | X | | | | | | | | | | | | | | | |
| Zoysia | | | | | | | | X | | | | | X | | | | X | | | | | | | |
| Buffalograss | | | | | | | | X | | | | | | | | | X | | | | | | | |
| Centipede | | | | | | | | X | | | | | | | | | X | | | | | | | |
| Bluegrass | | | | | X | | | | X | | | | | | | | | X | | | | X | | |
| Winter Lawn | | | | | | | | | | | | | (1 application, about 1 month after seeding) | | | | | | | | | | | |

These dates are approximate, but should be valid for most years for central and north Texas.

* Depending on length of growing season, an additional application may be needed in southern Texas. See Chapter 7 for more details.

125

# Quick Reference Guide
## Yearly Schedule

| | Jan. | Feb. | Mar. | Apr. | May | Jun. | Jul. | Aug. | Sep. | Oct. | Nov. | Dec. | See Chapter |
|---|---|---|---|---|---|---|---|---|---|---|---|---|---|
| Water if dry | X | X | X | X | X | X | X | X | X | X | X | X | 6 |
| Plant temporary lawns | X | X | X | | | | | | X | X | X | X | 13 |
| Weed Control (MSMA/DSMA) | | | | | X | X | X | X | X | | | | 8 |
| Seed tall fescue | | | X | X | | | | | | X | | | 4 |
| Mow | | | X | X | X | X | X | X | X | X | X | | 5 |
| Thatch control | | | X | | | | | | | | | | 12 |
| Seed bermuda | | | | X | X | X | X | X | | | | | 4 |
| Fertilize cool season | | | X | X | X | | | | | X | X | X | 7 |
| Fertilize warm season | | | | X | X | X | X | X | X | | | | 7 |
| Weed control pre-emergent | | | X | | | | | | X | | | | 8 |
| Weed control broadleaf | | | X | X | X | X | X | X | X | X | | | 8 |
| Winter weed control | X | X | X | | | | | | | | | | 8 |
| Lay sod | | | X | X | X | X | X | X | X | X | | | 4 |
| Aerification | | | | X | X | X | X | X | X | | | | 11 |
| Diseases | | | | X | X | X | X | X | X | | | | 10 |
| Insects | | | | | X | X | X | X | X | | | | 9 |

# GLOSSARY

**Aerification**—A mechanical process used to relieve the effects of soil compaction.

**Clippings**—Leaves cut off by mowing.

**Compaction**—The pressing together of soil particles by foot or vehicular traffic.

**Cool-season turfgrass**—Those turfgrasses primarily used in the Northern United States, such as Kentucky bluegrass, tall fescue and ryegrass.

**Coring**—Same as aerification.

**Cutting height**—The distance between the floor the mower is sitting on and the bed knife of a reel mower or the blade of a rotary mower.

**Dormant turf**—A brown-colored turf that has temporarily ceased growth due to unfavorable environmental conditions.

**Fertigation**—The application of fertilizer through an irrigation system.

**Fertilizer**—A liquid or dry material containing one or more of the essential plant nutrients.

**Foliar burn**—An injury to the leaves of the plant, caused by the application of a fertilizer or pesticide.

**Foot printing**—Discolored areas, or impressions, left in the lawn from foot traffic when the turf is in the first stage of wilt.

**French drain**—A drainage device in which a hole or trench is backfilled with sand or gravel.

**Fungicide**—A chemical used to control diseases caused by fungi.

**Grooving**—See vertical mowing.

**Herbicide**—A chemical used for weed control.

**Hydromulching**—A method of seeding using a mixture of seed, fertilizer and mulch, sprayed in a solution on the soil surface.

**Hydroseeding**—Same as hydromulching but without the mulch.

**Hydrosprigging**—Same as hydromulching but uses sprigs instead of seed.

**Insecticide**—A chemical used to control insects.

**Irrigation, automatic**—An irrigation system using pre-set timing devices.

**Mower, lapping**—Part of the process of sharpening a reel mower.

**Layering, soil**—An undesirable stratification of a soil.

**Localized dry spot**—An area of soil that resists wetting.

**Mat**—See thatch.

**Nematodes**—Small hair-like organisms that attack root systems.

**Overseeding**—Seeding a dormant turf with a cool-season grass in order to provide color during the winter.

**Pesticide**—A chemical used to control any turfgrass pest, such as weeds, insects and diseases.

**Plugging**—Establishing a turfgrass using plugs of sod.

**Reel mower**—A mower that cuts grass by means of a reel guiding the leaves against the cutting edge of the bedknife.

**Renovation**—Improving the vigor of a low-quality lawn.

**Rhizome**—A below-ground stem capable of producing a new plant.

**Rotary mower**—A mower that cuts grass with a high-speed blade that runs parallel to the soil surface.

**Scald**—Grass that dies under "standing water."

**Scalping**—The excessive removal of leaves during mowing, leaving mostly stems.

**Sod**—Plugs, squares or strips of turf with the adhering soil.

**Sprig**—See stolon.

**Sprigging**—Establishing a lawn using sprigs or stolons.

**Stolon**—An aboveground stem capable of growing a new plant.

**Thatch**—A layer of organic matter that develops between the soil and the base of the plant.

**Top-dressing**—Spreading a thin layer of soil on the lawn to smooth the surface.

**Transition zone**—An east-west zone through the middle of the U.S. between the northern area, growing cold-season turfgrasses, and the southern area, growing warm-season turfgrasses.

**Vertical mowing**—The use of mechanical device that has vertically rotating blades for thatch control.

**Warm season turfgrass**—Those turfgrasses used primarily in the southern United States, such as bermudagrass, St. Augustinegrass, zoysiagrass, centipedegrass and buffalograss.

**Wilt**—The discoloration and folding of leaves caused by either excessively dry or excessively wet conditions.

# INDEX